ANATOLE FRANCE
THE MAN AND HIS WORK

ANATOLE FRANCE EXAMINING A PRINT

From a drawing by Steinlen, engraved by Ernest Florian.
By permission of M. René Helleu

ANATOLE FRANCE
THE MAN AND HIS WORK
AN ESSAY IN CRITICAL BIOGRAPHY
BY JAMES LEWIS MAY
WITH ELEVEN ILLUSTRATIONS ❧

KENNIKAT PRESS
Port Washington, N. Y./London

ANATOLE FRANCE

First published in 1924
Reissued in 1970 by Kennikat Press
Library of Congress Catalog Card No: 70-103205
SBN 8046-0842-3

Manufactured by Taylor Publishing Company   Dallas, Texas

PREFACE

N the case of a writer like Anatole France, whose works present so many facets to humanity, it is difficult, if not impossible, to give a just appreciation of them all. The politician, for example, will be disposed to give predominance to Monsieur France's political *dicta;* the poet will prefer, to the exclusion of all others, those works in which his poetic genius is most conspicuously manifested; the satirist, again, will declare his predilection for those books in which irony plays the preponderating rôle. The difficulty of doing justice to so many-sided a writer is intensified when, as is the case with Anatole France, he is apt to change his point of view with such bewildering rapidity that often within the limits of a single chapter, sometimes of a single page, we find him playing all his parts in turn.

My own view, if I may venture to state it, is that the Anatole France who will outlive the rest, who will indeed endure so long as literature continues

v

to interest mankind, is Anatole France the poet. In saying this I am not, of course, referring only, or even principally, to his metrical compositions, but to that large body of work which, though prose in form, is poetic in inspiration and seems to recall by its subtle cadences that haunting Virgilian music which has ever affected him so profoundly and which he has praised so often and so well.

The life of Anatole France has not been rich in incident, but I have endeavoured to give, with the materials which his books afford and the personal details which he himself has supplied, a connected account of his career as a whole, but principally of his early and formative years.

In the second part of this essay, which deals with Monsieur France's works, it has not been my aim to give a detailed description of all the multifarious products of his pen. Adequately performed, such an undertaking would have far exceeded the limits of a single volume. I have but endeavoured to indicate, to those of my countrymen who are comparatively unacquainted with Monsieur France's work, the nature of those books which, in my opinion, are most characteristic of his genius.

The authorized English edition of Monsieur France's works is now becoming so well known that I have thought it well to quote the English titles throughout the following pages. I have, however,

added, at the end of the volume, for the convenience of such readers as may wish to refer to
the originals, a chronological list giving the French
and English titles in juxtaposition.

With little equipment save a sincere admiration
for the Master's works and a profound affection for
their writer, I should be foolish to hope that I had
come even within measurable distance of success in
a task which I am afraid not a few may regard as
unpardonably ambitious. Nevertheless, I shall not
deem myself wholly to have failed in my undertaking if, despite its manifold imperfections, this
monograph is found sufficiently persuasive to
prompt some of those into whose hands it may fall
to read and study for themselves the works of the
greatest living man of letters.

Among the many friends to whom my grateful
acknowledgments are due, I must make particular
mention of Monsieur Henry D. Davray, without
whose assistance and encouragement this book
would never have seen the light, and of Mr.
Holbrook Jackson, and Mr. Frederick Puller Sprent
of the British Museum, who have read the proofs
and offered many valuable suggestions.

CONTENTS

PART I—THE MAN

ix

LIST OF ILLUSTRATIONS

PART I

ANATOLE FRANCE
THE MAN

CHAPTER I

EARLY DAYS

"ONE of the most familiar legends in Brittany," says Renan in an immortal page, "tells of a supposed City of Is which, at some remote period of the world's history, is said to have been swallowed up by the sea. Divers places up and down the coast are pointed out as the site of the fabled city and strange are the stories concerning it that the fisher-folk will relate to you. On stormy days, they aver, you may catch a glimpse of its towers and turrets deep down in the trough of the waves, and when the winds are hushed there steals up through the deep waters the music of bells chiming out the canticle proper to the day. And to me it seems as though, in the depths of my heart, I too have a City of Is whose bells will not cease from ringing as they call to the sacred offices the faithful who no longer heed their summons. Sometimes I pause to listen to these tremulous vibrations, which seem to steal upon my inward ear from unfathomable depths, like voices from another

B

world. And now, especially, when old age is coming upon me, I have found a pleasure in recording the message of those far off murmurs of a vanished Atlantis."

It is, perhaps, something more than a coincidence that an author who owes so much to Renan, and who has exercised a profounder influence on educated minds throughout the world than any other French writer since Renan, should himself have lent an ear to those "tremulous vibrations" and have gathered up, within four imperishable volumes, his own *Souvenirs d'Enfance*, the memories of his early days and of the people, learned and simple, grave and gay, with whom, during childhood and adolescence, he was brought into familiar contact. They render the task of the biographer, at least for that period of his career, an easy one, for they are the faithful mirror of his mind and life—

> " *quo fit, ut omnis*
> *Votiva pateat veluti descripta tabella*
> *Vita senis.*"

Those four books, in which, giving himself the name of Pierre Nozière, Anatole France tells the story of his early days, are among the most subtly delicate things that have ever been written concerning the mind of a child. They are the record of those slight and often seemingly insignificant incidents which, nevertheless, exert so powerful and so permanent an influence on our lives, becoming, in Pater's phrase, " parts of the great chain wherewith we are bound." That the child is father to the man is true, in a measure, of all men, but especially is it true of Anatole France, and whoso would read his character aright, and understand his attitude towards life, must study with sympathetic attention the influences of his heredity and of his early environment.

Anatole France was born on April 16th, 1844, in a house on the Quai Malaquais which, with some others adjoining it, was subsequently pulled down to make room for the École des Beaux Arts. But though the house itself has vanished, its memory is enshrined in a beautiful passage of *My Friend's Book* in which Monsieur France tells of the room in which he used to sleep, and of the childish terrors which beset him there. " In this room," he says, " the most extraordinary adventures befell me. . . . No sooner had I lain down than the strangest individuals began to move in procession about me. They had noses like storks' bills, bristling moustaches, protuberant bellies and legs like chanticleer's. They came in, one after another, showing themselves in profile, each with a single goggle eye in the middle of his cheek, bearing brooms, skewers, guitars, squirts and other instruments that I knew not. . . . I never went to sleep. You can imagine one would not care to close one's eyes in such company as that, and I kept mine wide open. And yet, here is another marvel! I would suddenly find the room was flooded with sunlight and no one in it but my mother in her pink dressing-gown, and I could not for the life of me imagine how the night and the weird folk had vanished. 'What a boy you are to sleep,' my mother would say with a laugh." It was, too, of this house that he drew so beautiful and touching a picture in *The Crime of Sylvestre Bonnard*.

When it became necessary to quit the Quai Malaquais, the bookseller's business was removed to No. 9 Quai Voltaire, and it was here that Anatole France passed the greater part of his childhood and adolescence. This house, formerly the abode of the Baron Vivant Denon, diplomat and antiquary, subsequently passed into the possession of "le docte Honoré Champion," bookseller, and on his quitting it to take up his quarters at No. 5 Quai Malaquais, it was taken over by an upholsterer who has modernized it beyond recognition. In this house, then, his father, "le père France" as he was familiarly called, plied his trade as bookseller and denounced the shortcomings of the Republic. His real name was Thibault—François Noël Thibault—but the nickname France clung to him and was adopted by his son. We say nickname but, in reality, after a custom that still obtains in Anjou, it was merely an abbreviation of his first Christian name, François. This François Noël Thibault was a somewhat remarkable man. He was born at La Rue, a village or hamlet adjoining the market town of Saulgé l'Hôpital in Anjou on the 4 Nivose in the Year XIV—24th December, 1805. His father, Claude Pierre Thibault, carried on the business of shoemaker at Saulgé l'Hôpital, and on the 17th October, 1791, he had married Marie le Blanc, a young woman of his own commune. By her he had four children : Louis, Pierre, Véronique and François Noël. Louis, "Père Louis" as he was afterwards called, married and settled down in the district, where he was for many years a *garde champêtre*. He died in 1881. Of the other brother, Pierre, nothing is recorded save that he married in 1830. The town records contain no further trace of the name of François Noël Thibault until the 5th March, 1826, when he is mentioned as the first witness on the occasion of the birth of a nephew, Dominique Thibault. He is described, in the official entry, as François Noël Thibault, bachelor, aged 21, resident at Lignières, Commune de Brigné. It is noteworthy that the signature of François Noël does not appear on the register, but only those of the other two witnesses. In explanation of this circumstance it has been stated that, at

this period . of his career, the father of Anatole
France could neither read nor write. These accom-
plishments he taught himself during his military
service, which he voluntarily extended till the
year 1836 or 1837. As soon, however, as he had
learned to read he was seized with such a love of
books that on quitting the army he set up as a
bookseller on the *Quais*. He married, and lived successively at No. 16 Rue de Seine-Saint-Germain,
No. 19 Quai Malaquais, the birthplace of his son
Anatole, and No. 9 Quai Voltaire. At length, in
1878, he retired to Neuilly sur Seine. Despite his
voluntary exile from the home of his forbears,
François Noël never forgot Anjou or his family.
" I am always pleased," he writes in a letter dated
13th June, 1841, to his brother Louis Thibault the
garde champêtre, " to learn that all my family are
well and prospering. Our mother, too, is well.
. . . She is, even now, tougher than any of us;
they tell me she is as young as ever. Please tell
mother that my wife would like her to stand godmother to her child; you do not know perhaps
that it is expected between the 15th and 20th July.
Mind you tell the poor old mother that she would
be very fond of her daughter-in-law if she knew
her. She has all the qualities that go to the making
of a good wife.

" Your brother, France, bookseller."

In another letter dated 17th June, 1878, " Père France," now a septuagenarian, writes from Neuilly to his nephew who had been there to pay him a visit and makes the following allusion to his son Anatole : " If you want to read the articles of your cousin Anatole, there are some in *Le Temps* of the 12th and 15th June. You would be able to see this paper in the reading room at Angers."

In the shop of the elder France, who was a devout Catholic and a staunch upholder of the Monarchy, there foregathered many of the greatest writers and most original thinkers of the day, and the young alumnus of the Collège Stanislas must have been the silent listener to many a discussion afterwards re-echoed in the philosophic outpourings of the Abbé Jérôme Coignard or the scholarly disquisitions of Monsieur Bergeret.

It is necessary clearly to bear in mind the peasant strain which Anatole France inherited from his father, if we would form a just estimate of his character and temperament. Hitherto it has, perhaps, been taken insufficiently into account. Because the overtly expressed convictions and opinions of the son, a sceptic and a democrat, are diametrically opposed to those of his Catholic and Royalist father, it has been rather rashly inferred that the paternal strain was a negligible factor, and that there was nothing in common between father and son. Some *prima facie* support is lent to this assumption by Anatole France himself, who tells us that he generally formed his opinions on any given subject by taking the view that was diametrically opposed to his father's. But the operations of the intellect are often artificial and sometimes superficial in character. *Non in dialectica complacuit Deo salvum facere populum suum* says St. Ambrose, and Anatole France has more than once expressed his scorn of human reason. But the instincts are deep and elemental and there are many indications in the character of Anatole France that he is indebted, in no small degree, for his visionary cast of mind, for an almost morbid faculty of seeing ghosts where common-sense folk see nothing, to the peasant blood in his veins. The cradle of the Thibault family was in the department of the Maine-et-Loire, some five miles from Brissac, in the commune of Saulgé l'Hôpital. "The circumstance is not without significance," says M. G. A. Masson, "and there is reason to believe that Anatole France received at birth from one of those judicious fairies, who preside with such wisdom over the laws of heredity, a little of that ' douceur angevine ' which so melodiously modulated the poetry of Joachim du Bellay."

Anatole France is currently represented as a past-master in the art of irony, the most genial mocker of our day. This is true, but it is only part of the

truth. He is certainly an ironist and a mocker;
but he is a poet and a visionary as well. In a
strange little story which, with its suggestion of
the mysterious and supernatural, is singularly remi-
niscent of Edgar Allen Poe, he recounts how he
rode out, one bleak December night, on some
family business, to visit a certain house—at that
time untenanted—which had sheltered his father's
ancestors for more than two hundred years. He
put up for the night at the village inn, and while
waiting for a frugal supper which the landlady,
who was old and hideously ugly, grudgingly con-
sented to prepare, he sat meditating in front of the
fire. " I was," he says, " weary and low-spirited,
weighed down with an indescribable sense of mental
oppression. Thick-coming fancies, scenes of violence
and gloom, tormented my imagination. After a
while I fell into a fitful doze, but in my uneasy
slumber I could hear the moaning of the wind in
the chimney, and now and again a gust of more
than usual violence would fling the ashes from the
hearth over my very boots.

" When, a few moments afterwards, I opened my
eyes, I beheld a sight that I shall never forget. I
saw at the far end of the room, silhouetted with
the utmost distinctness against the whitewashed
wall, a motionless shadow—the shadow of a young
girl. The form was so instinct with gentleness,

purity and charm that, as I beheld it, I felt all my weariness, all my melancholy, melt away into wonder and delight.

"Next day I went and looked at the empty house . . . I scoured the neighbourhood; I cross-questioned the *curé;* but I learned nothing that would enable me to discover the identity of the young girl whose ghost I had seen. Perhaps there, in the bleak solitudes of Le Bocage, some phantom had been wont to appear to those peasants whose descendant I am, and maybe it was the ancestral ghost which haunted of old my untutored, dreamy forefathers, that presented itself with unwonted grace to the gaze of their visionary child."

But besides the gift of second sight, if such we may term it, that the boy owed to his father's side of the family, there is another characteristic for which he was indebted to the bookseller of the Quai Voltaire, and that is his total lack of the commercial instinct. That little boy who asked his mother whether it was the people who bought or the people who sold that pay the money, that little boy of whom his mother prophesied that he would never know the value of money, doubtless derived this disability from the bookseller who, according to his son, was much more interested in the reading of books than in the selling of them. Avarice, in the estimation of Anatole France, is the unloveliest, the least forgivable, of all the vices, and this disregard of money, this contempt for meanness in any shape or form, he inherited from that up-holder of lost causes, the ex-guardsman of Charles X.

Though the parents of the young Anatole were not in straitened circumstances, they were assuredly not rich. We may be permitted to suppose—in fact it is pretty plainly hinted, *passim*, in the Nozière tetralogy—that the father was much more interested in ideas, in questions of politics and religion, than in his business, and that he would far rather overcome an adversary in argument than get the better of him in a commercial transaction. Such proclivities might have spelt financial disaster to the business had they not been to a great extent modified and counterbalanced by the vigilant eye of the mother, to whom the practical common sense of the household evidently belonged. Madame Thibault was of Flemish extraction, and the im-pression, or rather the series of impressions, which Monsieur France gives us of his mother, is wholly charming. To begin with, she was, as we have said, eminently practical; she was the keen, bright and most salutary foil to a theorizing husband altogether too prone to mount upon the airy stilts of abstraction. She had that faculty which is seen in its supreme development in the women of France and Scotland, the faculty of looking after the gear. And she was

devoted to her little boy. She recounted to him
the lives of the saints, for she was a devout, church-
going woman. She told him stories which he in
turn has told to us, and, though she sang to no one
else, she sang to him. She was gentle and soft-
hearted with her domestics and all who served her;
her manners were characterized by simplicity and
reserve; she was not without a touch of feminine
pride in her personal appearance, she did not disdain the vain and perishable graces; she was as
dainty and pretty as she was kind. The child
adored her and feared no ill when she was by.

A French critic has justly observed that, if
children always resembled their parents, there is a
considerable likelihood that *La Rôtisserie de la Reine
Pédauque* would never have been written. It often
happens, however, that they take after their grand-
parents, and in the portrait Monsieur France has
drawn for us of his father's mother we recognize
those traits of indulgent humour, genial mockery,
and gentle irony that are so conspicuously characteristic of himself. " Grandmamma was frivolous;
yes, Grandmamma's ideas about morality were not
of the strictest; Grandmamma had no more piety
in her composition than a bird. You ought to
have seen the little quizzical grimace she would
make on Sundays when Mother and I were setting
out for church. She used to smile at the seriousness

ANATOLE FRANCE
AGED 6
From a miniature by Mlle Stéphanie Goblin

which my mother brought to bear on everything
connected with this world and the next. She
readily forgave me my faults and I think she would
have forgiven bigger ones than mine."

Clearly, it was to her that Anatole France owed
his tolerance, his gentle mocking irony, his humour,
his tenderness, his breadth of sympathy, his keen
sense of the absurd, his indulgence and compassion.

Such then were the people in whose intimacy the
boy grew up. He was an only child and, after the
manner of such children, he was perhaps too much
petted, too much thrown in upon himself. Like
Charles Lamb, to whom, in some respects of his
life, he bears so striking an affinity, he was let loose
in a library, reading and musing, musing and reading,
" *in angello cum libello.*" Of an evening, while his
mother was busy with her needlework, he would
turn over the pages of his picture Bible, beneath
the lamp that shed a glow of infinite sweetness.
Given to reverie and day-dreaming, losing himself
in a brown study, imaginative and rather wayward,
the child grew up in sheltered solitude, his sole
contact with the outer world being the daily walks
he took with his old nurse, Madame Mathias, whom
he dearly loved. " Ah, Madame Mathias, Madame
Mathias," he cried in later years, " what would I
not give to see you once again in your habit as you
lived, or at least to know what fate has been yours

these thirty years that have gone by since you quitted this world. . . . Could I but have tidings of you now, what deep content, what infinite peace would be mine. Into that lowly coffin wherein you vanished from our sight that fair spring morning . . . you bore with you countless things that were mine no less than yours; things that touched the heart, a whole world of ideas brought into being by the association of your old age and my childhood. What have you done with them, Madame Mathias? Do you bethink yourself, in the region where you are tarrying now, of the long walks we used to take together, you and I ? "

At length the time came for the child to quit nurse and governess and to go to school, and he was sent to the Collège Stanislas, where it cannot be said that he was happy. Mass instruction, he tells us, was ill suited to his disposition; competitive examinations, the system of rewards and punishments, he found unnatural and degrading. " From my childhood onward," he says, " I have always been in love with solitude, the thought of a glade in a wood, of a rivulet in a meadow, was enough to send me, as I sat there on my form, into transports of desire and love and longing that almost amounted to despair. Perhaps I should have fallen sick with grief in that dreadful school had I not been saved by a gift which I have retained all through my life, the gift of seeing the comic side of things." His masters, by their eccentricities and absurdities, provided him with the distractions of a comedy. They were unwittingly " his Molières." But the school from which he derived most profit was his beloved Paris itself, its busy streets with their stir and bustle, its noble buildings, the manifold activities of its citizens as they went to and fro, the shop windows, the various trades and handicrafts. He is no lover of the boarding-school system, and the *internes* have the full measure of his compassion. " The family board, with its fair white cloth, its clear sparkling decanters, the tranquil faces, the easy, natural talk—from all these things a boy may learn to love and understand the lowly and hallowed elements of human life. If he is fortunate enough to have, as I had, kindly and intelligent parents, the table talk to which he listens will give balance to his mind and dispose his heart to love. . . . Meals taken in boarding-school refectories have not this sweetness and this grace. Ah, Home is a famous school ! "

All this is perhaps somewhat hard doctrine for an Englishman to digest, but it must be borne in mind that a boarder in a French *lycée* enjoys a far smaller measure of freedom and independence than an English public school boy. Putting aside every temptation to discuss the rival merits of the systems

—the English and the French—it is probable that
Anatole France, with his reserved and timid nature,
his dreaminess, his love of solitude and his dislike
of games, was hardly fitted for the rough and tumble
of public school life. " I perceived," he tells us,
" that I was somehow different from others, without
knowing whether that difference was for my good
or ill, and the feeling perturbed me." His tastes,
his thoughts, his attitude towards his fellows were
different from those of the average boy, and abnor-
mality is not a popular thing in a school. Dreamers,
as Joseph discovered to his cost, run a grave risk of
being unpopular with their fellows and with those
in authority over them. And so it was with the
boy France. While his masters were endeavouring
to pound the classics into him in such a manner as
to get him through his *baccalauréat* with credit,
he was lost in contemplation of the visions his
reading summoned up before his inward eye.
" Sophocles, Euripides," he cries, " they opened the
gates of an enchanted world to me. To the *Alcestis*
and the *Antigone* I owe the noblest dreams that ever
schoolboy was visited by. As I sat at my ink-
stained desk, my head buried in my dictionary,
forms of godlike beauty passed before my vision;
I beheld arms of gleaming ivory falling upon snowy
tunics; I heard voices sweeter than the sweetest
melody mourning most musically."

It is small wonder that his name figured but rarely on the prize lists. Pupils of his type are seldom in favour with their masters. But dreams Monsieur Anatole France holds to be of vital necessity to a man. " Receive," he cried forty years ago to " Marcelle of the Golden Eyes," his godmother, his fairy, " receive the blessing of him whom, as a little child, thou didst gather in thine arms to behold the colour of his eyes. On him thou didst bestow the rarest of thy gifts, O most generous heart; for, opening thine arms to him, thou madest him free of the illimitable land of dreams." And, in this respect at least, he has not changed. " I love Truth," he says in the epilogue of his latest book, " I believe that man has need of it; but assuredly he has still greater need of the illusions that encourage and console, that set no limit to his hopes and aspirations. Rob him of his illusions, and man would perish of very weariness and despair."

Maybe, but the dreamer must look for no reward beyond his dreams. His kingdom knows no bourn, but it may not be bartered for a single rood of earthly soil. Which is to say that, while the young Anatole was in his Paradise of dreams, the others were poring diligently over their paradigms and " satisfying the examiners." It is characteristic of this *enfant rêveur* that when he was sitting for his *baccalauréat* he spent his luncheon hour musing on

c

the towers of Notre-Dame. When he came to earth, he had missed his turn for the *viva voce*, a thing without precedent in the recollection of the oldest beadle in the Sorbonne. No, at school his dreams did not win him marks, or only bad ones.

But over and beyond the family circle, the book-shop and its customers and the Collège Stanislas, there was yet another influence, less obvious perhaps, less direct, in its operation, but certainly not less potent or less permanent in its results. It was the influence of the City of Paris. And indeed it would have been strange if one who had so great an admiration for beautiful things, who deemed that the only unpardonable offences were offences against beauty, had not received the indelible imprint of that gracious *paysage lapidaire*. Educationists who hold that what enters at the eye may be at least of equal importance with what enters at the ear, will perhaps not taunt us with stating something over-fanciful or far-fetched if we detect in the orderliness, the tranquillity, the distinction of Monsieur France's style—which after all is but the mirror of his mind— the reflection, as it were, of the beautiful city in whose bosom he was nurtured. Anatole France is a Parisian. Scattered broadcast up and down his writings are passages which tell of the intimate, understanding love which he bears the city of whose past he is so reverently proud, for whose future he nourishes such lofty ideals. As Lamb was essentially a Londoner, so France is essentially a Parisian. A Parisian born, a Parisian he has remained, and no lover ever praised his mistress's charms in choicer phrases than those in which Anatole France belauds the beauties of his beloved Paris. " How delicious," he says, " was the joy with which I used to breathe in the light which floods those regions of storied elegance, the Tuileries, the Louvre and the Palais Mazarin . . . the tumbled heights of Chaillot, the Trocadero hill, then still a wilderness starred with moon-daisies and fragrant with wild thyme. But what I knew the best and loved the best were the banks of the Seine, whither my old nurse Nanette used to take me day by day."

Paris was the book wherein he read his history.

" If ever the consciousness of being a son of this city of generous ideals thrilled me with delight, it was when I took my walks along those quays whose very stones, from the Palais Bourbon to Notre-Dame, are eloquent of the story of one of the most glorious adventures of the human spirit, the story of the France that was and of the France that is to-day. There stands the Louvre glittering like a jewel, there the Pont Neuf. . . . The whole genius of France has passed in long succession over those venerable arches whose carven faces, some wreathed in smiles, some grim and forbidding, seem to symbolise the suffering and the glory, the hopes and the fears, the loves and the hates of which they have been the silent witnesses through the centuries."

Such, then—the home, the school, the city— were the three main influences that moulded the boyhood of Anatole France and made him what he was when, shaking the dust of the Sorbonne from off his feet, he stood on the threshold of the big world.

His life exhibits, at least on the surface, many seeming contrarieties. In reality it is, as we hope to show, strangely consistent. Indulgent pity for the follies and the weaknesses of men, a poignant consciousness of the frailty and evanescence of earthly things, a profound sense of the vanity of human endeavour, of the obscurity of man's destiny, of the *lacrimæ rerum*, the pathos of life, these are the deep underlying traits of his character. His mockery, his irony, are but a mask veiling a face that looks out upon the world with eyes of infinite compassion, or perhaps we should say that, if he laughs, he laughs like Figaro, lest he should be betrayed into the weakness of tears. If Irony and Pity are the keynotes of his character, the Irony he invokes, as he himself tells us in his own *Garden of Epicurus*, is no cruel deity. She mocks neither love nor beauty. She is gentle and kindly disposed. She is, indeed, hardly distinguishable from Pity herself. If, then, we would find the key to the enigma presented by the intellectual evolution of Anatole France, if we would understand by what steps the author of *My Friend's Book* and *The Crime of Sylvestre Bonnard* came to be the author of *The Church and the Republic, Towards Better Days*, and *Penguin Island ;* if we would understand how the sceptic became the partisan, the dreamer the man of action; if we would grasp how the modest and retiring scholar came forth from his retreat to castigate the politicians, if we would understand how this urbane and meditative disciple of Epicurus who so deeply loved " retired leisure " came to leave his Tower of Ivory, and to take part in the debates of the noisy throng for whose contact he had always betrayed so profound an aversion, we must seek the explanation of these and all the other apparent anomalies and contradictions of his character in the compassionate idealism by which he is constantly animated and which sounded so peremptorily in his ear.

CHAPTER II

ADOLESCENCE

THE first stage of the journey is now nearly accomplished. The school days are all but over. Monsieur France, as we have seen, has many complaints to make against his preceptors and against the system which they had to carry out. Now, it is an almost universal experience to look forward to leaving school with pleasure, and to look back upon it with regret. This was the case with Anatole France. " I was very unhappy," he says, " at school, almost constantly so, and I thought I was in for a splendid time when I left. But when, at length, I issued from its walls never to return, I was not so happy as I had anticipated." He then proceeds to blame the system. In the ears of Anatole France, the mere sound of the word " System " is as odious as it was pleasant in those of the elder Feverel. Now systems, aiming at ensuring the greatest common measure of benefit, are necessarily rigid in their application, and occasionally unhappy, even tragic, in their results. They are designed to apply to average humanity. The experience of such as fall outside that category, the abnormally sensitive, for example, or the abnormally gifted, is not likely to be peculiarly happy. To the majority of boys, life at school means just so much " stuff " to master, to get up, in order that they may pass their examinations and so proceed to the career that they have in view : medicine, the services, business, or whatever it may be. Literature to them is but a means to an end. Of Homer, Virgil, Horace and the rest, it is necessary to acquire a certain amount of knowledge for a certain definite object. The average boy considers that, on the whole, the thing is rather a bore, and, unless he is a prig, he is at no pains to disguise his sentiments. In English schools, at any rate, enthusiasms of any kind, but particularly enthusiasms for intellectual things, are often looked upon as rather bad form.

It occasionally happens, however, that there wanders into the fold a youngling of an order so different from the common herd that his presence is an embarrassment alike to the shepherds and to the rest of the flock. Strangely and unaccountably dispensed from serving that preliminary apprentice-ship to life which Newman declares to be a necessary antecedent condition to a due understanding of the classics, our *rara avis*, our irritating exception, is already endowed with what his masters are very

unlikely to possess : an ear sensitively attuned to
the music that sounds eternally—for those who can
hear it—in the great poetic masterpieces of Greece
and Rome. Such boys are apt to fall a-dreaming
and to be contemplating visions when they ought
to be attending to the work of the class. This was
a proclivity to which the boy Anatole was grievously
addicted. Fortunately he was never cured of it.
" I saw Thetis," he tells us in *My Friend's Book*,
" rising like a white cloud from the sea; I saw
Nausicaa and her maidens, the palm-tree of Delos,
and the sky and the land and the sea; and I saw
Andromache smiling through her tears . . . I
understood—I felt it all. For six months I was lost
in the Odyssey. It earned me many punishments.
. . . But I deserved them all! I was occupying
myself with matters extraneous to the work of the
class. Alas, the habit has clung to me! In whatever class in life's school they put me for the rest of
my days, I am afraid that, old man though I be, I
shall still incur the rebukes I received as a boy at
the hands of my professor : ' Monsieur Pierre
Nozière, your mind is occupied with matters
extraneous to the work of the class ! ' " But it was
not only in the class-room that he was thus given
to day-dreaming. The habit with him was inveterate. On his way home he would stay his
steps by flaring shop-windows to con a line or two

and then recite them in an undertone as he pursued his way. " Often enough," he said, " I collided with a baker's boy with his basket on his head, dreaming his dreams as I was dreaming mine; or else I would suddenly feel on my cheek the hot breath of some unlucky horse tugging at his load. . . . One evening I read some lines of the *Antigone* by the lantern of a vendor of baked chestnuts, and even now, after a quarter of a century, I can never think of the line that begins

O tomb ! O bridal bed !

without seeing the man of Auvergne blowing into a paper bag, or feeling my side grow warm with the heat of the stove where his chestnuts were a-roasting."

Monsieur France has some hard things to say about his Dominies; but he was probably not an easy case. The riotous, the rebellious, the contumacious, the dull, the lazy, the clever, the cunning, these are types commonly to be met with; they are to be expected; they are in the natural order of things and are to be treated on certain traditional lines. But that a boy should be, not indeed clever—Anatole France was emphatically not that—but a genius—*that* is almost a species of affront and is calculated to arouse resentment. We can imagine the scene at the Collège Stanislas : the boy France with his mind far away on the shores of Hellas gazing

out over the wine-dark sea, or marching with the
Roman legionaries to victory or disaster—we can
imagine him suddenly called upon to go on con-
struing, standing up in confusion, fumbling un-
successfully for the place, and finally given an
" impot " for being an incorrigible wool-gatherer.
How different, this, from the type of the smart,
efficient, successful, cocksure schoolboy whom
Monsieur France has portrayed under the name of
Fontanet, Fontanet who possessed just that measure
of hypocrisy necessary to ensure his success in
the world. Fontanet was " up to the mark " in
everything he did, he never got into scrapes himself,
he merely instigated wrong-doing in others, or,
if he entered upon some questionable enterprise as
a confederate, he disembarked in good time to avoid
the breakers. He had a characteristic appreciation
of the value of money, which Anatole France never
had. When, for example, the two boys formed a
fund for the relief of the deserving poor, it was
Fontanet who constituted himself Treasurer. " He
imbued me," says his partner, " with the notion that
some day or other his aunt, who was very rich, would
give two or three times as much as my contribution,
and that, in the meantime, I ought to entrust the
seven shillings and fourpence halfpenny to his
keeping. This transfer, according to him, was
necessary for the proper administration of the

Fund's accounts." To Fontanet and to all his tribe,
Anatole France offered a marked contrast. Though
he was guaranteed from going down to the last three
places, " that position being assured in perpetuity
to Morlot, Laboriette and Chazal," it is nevertheless the fact that he had " an innate tendency
to descend "; a hidden and malign influence inclined
him towards the lower strata. " I grew sad," he
says, " at this progressive deterioration and sought
in vain for its cause, it never dawning upon me to
ascribe it to the fact that I took no account of what
was said and done in class." But Fortune plays
some strange tricks, even in clerical schools, yet few
as strange as when, one unforgettable Saturday,
she brought Anatole France out " top " in Latin
composition. Monsieur Beaussier, the master, was
a just man. His Themis was devoid of illumination
and grace, but she kept his scales of justice even.
" He made the announcement of my success in a
grave voice, with an air of sadness and profound
dejection. He gave the impression that the thing
was annoying, that it was regrettable, that it was
immoral. But at any rate he announced it, he
proclaimed it, and that very place in which it
pained him to see me installed, he himself ordained
that I should occupy. The composition, it appears,
was difficult. The cleverest had gone astray in
several passages. They had sought and found not.

But my very heedlessness had been my best friend. As was usual with me, I had gone straight ahead, without thinking at all. And, not perceiving the difficulties in my path, I had surmounted them all. Such, at all events, was the wide solution hazarded by Monsieur Beaussier of the inexplicable circumstance. Whatever the explanation, I had come out top."

It was not for long, however, that the dreamer was destined to occupy the eminence to which his very ignorance had thus fortuitously raised him. Nor, it must be confessed, were his dreams invariably of the scenes and personages of antiquity. They were sometimes less idealistic, less nebulous, and on one occasion his obsession with the charms of a certain Mademoiselle Isabelle Constant, an actress who had played the part of Margaret of Scotland at his first theatre, so seriously interfered with his ability to define the distinction between the three voices of the Greek verb that, when he was called upon to state the precise meaning of παρασκεθέσθαι, he " sat looking like a fool and said nothing."

His dreaming propensity accompanied him up to the very last stage of his school career. When he was up for his *baccalauréat* his mother—as is the wont of mothers in such circumstances—gave him some money to have his lunch near the Sorbonne,

presumably so that he should not have to walk all
the way home and back. But—as is the wont of
sons in such circumstances—he kept the money,
bought himself a few biscuits and went and ate them
on the Towers of Notre-Dame. " There," he says,
" I reigned over Paris. The Seine flowed on amid
the housetops, domes and towers, and the eye
followed it into the blue distance till the silver
thread of it was lost among the green hills. Beneath
my feet lay fifteen hundred years of glory and great
deeds, of crime and misery, an ample subject for
my yet unformed and unpractised mind to meditate
upon. I know not of what I stayed there dreaming,
but when I arrived within the gates of the old
Sorbonne I had missed my turn."

These school-day reminiscences of Anatole France
contain some unforgettable portraits of masters and
boys that are as living, and touched with as
delicate a humour, as those pictures which Lamb
has drawn of the quaint inhabitants of the old
South Sea House. There was Monsieur Crottu,
whose mind was as ugly as his body ; Crottu the
crabbed, Crottu the unjust. " Wretched creature
that he was, a thick hide covered his short fat hands
which dishonoured everything on which their heavy
clumsiness descended, and which could bring him
no delight from any pleasurable contact. His
shifty eyes knew not how to linger on objects of

loveliness. His countenance was joyless, and the only indication of pleasure he ever allowed himself was to put out his slobbering tongue as he recorded his unhallowed penalties within his grimy register."

Immortal, too, is Monsieur Mésange—or as we might say Mr. Thomas Titmus—the mathematical master. A witty scholar and a promising Latinist wrote a poem in flowing hexameters on the metamorphosis of this gentleman into the bird whose name he bore. No name could have been more tragically inappropriate, for Monsieur Mésange was doomed to carry, in this transitory life, an immense, amorphous body of portentous adiposity by whose iniquitous burden he was nearly crushed to the ground. This crude and inchoate mass was perpetually dripping with sweat. Moreover, it exuded a warm steamy mist highly agreeable to flies. But Nature in her thoughtlessness had furnished this monstrous trunk with a child's arms, so that it was only with difficulty that Monsieur Mésange could keep off the winged insects which came in swarms to batten on his oleaginous cranium. And while he was instilling into his pupils the properties of numbers, he would contemplate with envious eye the little birds as they pecked the bread crumbs in the playground.

You ask whether these personages are real or imaginary? " Reader," says Charles Lamb at the

THE COLLÈGE STANISLAS
From a photograph

conclusion of his essay on the South Sea House, " what if I have been playing with thee all this while—peradventure the very *names*, which I have summoned up before thee, are fantastic—insubstantial—like Henry Pimpernel and old John Naps of Greece :—Be satisfied that something answering them has had a being." And similarly Anatole France in the Epilogue to *The Bloom of Life* says, " I have invented details to replace circumstances that had escaped me, but those inventions never had any other purpose than to reveal and illustrate a character. In short, I believe that no one ever lied with a greater regard for the truth." And indeed they bear the stamp of verisimilitude upon them. Some personages there were whose mode of life he has set down without the smallest alteration or disguise, retaining even their real names. Such for example was Monsieur Dubois, scholar and gentleman of the Old School, antiquary, friend and counsellor of the France family. If we dwell at some length on Dubois— whose full name was Dubois-Dubès—it is because to him, more than to anyone else, certainly more than to any of his schoolmasters, Anatole France is indebted for those tastes and ideas, that love of classic elegance, of austere refinement which has left its indelible imprint upon his literary style. In a few deft, incisive strokes Anatole France brings him before us in his habit as he lived. He was " a tall old man of seventy or seventy-two who held his head erect, bowed with elegance, and displayed a manner which was at once affable and reserved. He wore his hair brushed straight up and a pair of short side whiskers, trimmed after the fashion of his youth, relieved his long, smooth visage. His features were severe, his smile charming. He usually wore a long bottle-green frock-coat, took snuff from an oval tortoise-shell snuff-box and blew his nose in an enormous red bandana. If I had not heard Monsieur Dubois discussing matters with my father, with whose opinions on every conceivable subject he disagreed; if I had never seen him paying his devoirs to my mother, who was too artless and too shy to encourage elaborate addresses, I should never have imagined the pitch of perfection to which a man of refined breeding can bring the art of good behaviour and courteous reserve." Descended from well-to-do professional people, barristers, magistrates under the old *régime*, Monsieur Dubois, from his upbringing and associations, belonged to the old courtly school of French society. He was a man of settled habits, who loved and practised simplicity, making it at once a pleasure and a virtue. He loved Virgil—he knew his Virgil by heart—and he disliked Napoleon. He was not only learned, but a thinker, a philosopher, with original and well defined ideas. He held schools and scholastic curricula in small esteem. He used to tease Madame France; he was what people of the Victorian era used to call a " quiz "; " but," says Anatole France, " it was because he was fond of my mother that he used to single her out as the object of his provoking humour. We only tease the people we love." Though he often shocked her with his views on religion and morality, which were not so strict as his views on grammar, Madame France had great respect for him, and often sought his advice concerning the government of participles, which were a great worry to her, and of her son, who was a still greater. One week the boy's report was lamentable, " Conduct—bad. Progress—nil." Madame France, in great distress, besought Monsieur Dubois to admonish him. " Since you are kind enough to take an interest in the child," said she, " give him a scolding. He will pay more heed to you than to me. Make him understand the harm he is doing himself by neglecting his studies."

" How would you have me make him recognize this harm," answered Monsieur Dubois, " if I do not recognize it myself ? "

And, producing a volume from his pocket, he read these lines :

" Homer did not spend ten years boxed up in a school to be whipped into learning a few words

D

which he could have learnt better at home in five or six months."

" And do you know who said that, Madame ? A clown, think you, an ignoramus, an enemy of learning ? No, it was a gentle soul, a very learned man, the best writer of his time—the time of Chateaubriand—a witty satirist, a lover of Greek, the man who so charmingly translated the pastoral of *Daphnis and Chloe*, the man who wrote the most delightful letters in the world : it was Paul Louis Courier."

My mother gazed at Monsieur Dubois with an expression of pained surprise ; and the old man, gently pulling me by the ear, said :

" My friend, it is not enough merely to be deaf to these learned prigs, the enemies of Nature ; you must hearken to the voice of Nature herself, for only she can teach you to understand Virgil and instruct you in the law of numbers. Lose not a moment, when you are free, in making up for the time you have to waste at school."

A pupil of the renowned Clavier, Monsieur Dubois was a great admirer of Winckelmann, and lent young Anatole France the works of that illustrious antiquary, over which he pored till he began to lose his colour. It was Monsieur Dubois who, as he turned the pages of his book, would lean over him and give him valuable lessons that he never forgot, making him think, as he calls them to mind, of that group so often reproduced which portrayed the musical Satyr teaching a young Faun how to play the Syrinx. "Intellectually," says Anatole France, "he was the greatest man I had ever known, the greatest I was ever destined to know throughout the course of my long life, and yet I have been friendly with people whose writings have made them famous. But the example of Monsieur Dubois and of a few others who, like him, left no works to perpetuate their name, has made me suspect that the highest human worth has often perished without leaving a trace behind it."

Anatole France was slow to acquire knowledge, but what he did acquire he retained. As a scholar, he tells us, he was always "a day behind the fair." He congratulates himself thereon, for it prevented him from grinding for those examinations which do such grievous harm to the brain. It enabled him to keep the bloom of freshness on his ideas. "Certainly," he confesses, "such a condition of mind was ill-adapted to benefit by mass teaching, which addresses itself solely to the memory, to the mechanical memory and not to the æsthetic memory, not to the divine Mnemosyne from whom the Muses spring." And then he adds characteristically, "Let us beware : perhaps even as I say these things there yet lingers in my heart some trace, some vestige of rancour against Fontanet, whose memory, swift as Cæsar's victories, triumphant and arrogant, filled me with envy and admiration."

And so he gradually grew up. The picture Bible, the family board, his nurses Nanette, Madame Mathias and Mélanie, the nursery governess who set him to read La Fontaine while she wrote letters to her young man, the Collège Stanislas with Crottu, Brard and Beaussier, his masters, and the streets with their everyday sights and sounds that revealed the working of the social machine, and the gracious city with its beautiful and historic buildings, the gentle flowing river, the quays with their boxes of mouldering books " silently expressing old mortality, the ruins of forgotten times "—such were the influences, or some of them, amid which this delicate, half-spoiled, wayward, indolent child of genius grew to adolescence. Beginning by looking on the world and its inhabitants as a box of toys, the day soon came when an old man's tragic death—he threw himself in a fit of delirium from a garret in the Frances' house, in which he lived—rudely put an end to this pleasant illusion. " From that day onwards, I ceased, once and for all, to look upon life as a pastime, or upon the world as a box of toys. My theory of the universe had been shovelled away with old, forgotten, exploded things; it had gone to dwell with the Ptolemaic system and the map of the world as the ancients knew it, in the Limbo of Human Errors." Sorrow, he says somewhere, is the great instructress, and slowly and surely he learned how large a part sorrow and suffering play in life, so that it is with a sad smile that he recalls, in one of his stories, that universal epitome of the life of man, "They are born, they suffer and they die." He early caught the eternal note of sadness that sounds for ever on the shores of human life.

During all these early years he, like Shakespeare, did tread on earth unguessed at. His mother, of course, thought him a genius. Mothers always think thus of their sons. His father took a different view. He formed what the financiers are wont to call a conservative estimate of his son's capabilities. Without being a milksop—he was anything but that—Anatole France was evidently a mother's boy. With his father's views he invariably disagreed. The circumstance is not uncommon. The father probably wanted to see his son's name figure with regularity on the school prize lists. He expected him to be marked as first-rate in conduct, diligence and progress; and "conduct—bad; progress—nil" must have grievously disappointed him. The elder France was a man of intelligence. He looked on his son's achievements in the light of reason and formed no extravagant hopes. The mother looked upon them in the light of love which illumined the

pathways of the future.   When in the course of his
school career he was called upon to " bifurcate," or,
as we should say, to elect whether he would specialize
on the Classical or the Modern side, his parents did
not help him with their advice.   " The principal
reason why they said nothing was that my mother
never doubted that, whatever line I followed, my
genius was bound to make itself felt in the long run ;
whereas my father deemed that whether I ' opted '
for Literature or for Science I should never do any
good at either."   Maternal instinct is a better guide
than paternal reason.   Madame France even went
counter to Monsieur Dubois, who had enjoined the
boy never to think of being an author ; for, he said,
the literary career was one in which moderate success
was less desirable than downright failure.   As soon
as Monsieur Dubois' back was turned, she kissed her
son on the nape of his neck and whispered in his
ear :

" Be a writer, my son ; you have brains, and you
will make the envious hold their tongues."

And now then at length the long school days are
over ; the Collège Stanislas will know him as a
scholar no more, and no more, with his satchel
under his arm, will he trip his way " merry as a
sparrow " across the Jardin du Luxembourg.   He
is promoted to a room of his own.   Hitherto he had
slept either in a sort of box-room adjoining the

drawing-room and too small for the door to be shut
at night, or else in the dressing-room, which was
filled with a lumber of superfluous furniture. But
now that he had a room, *his* room, he began
to live a life of his own; he was conscious of an
inward existence. " Poor little room of my childhood days," he cries, in the beautiful conclusion to
Little Pierre, " it was within your four walls that
there began slowly to gather round me the many-
hued shadows of knowledge, all those illusions that
have hidden Nature from my sight and gathered
more and more densely between myself and her as
I increased my efforts to unveil her mystery. It
was there, within your four narrow walls, with their
garland of blue flowers, that there appeared to me,
at first faint and far-off, the terrifying simulacra of
Love and Beauty."

Well then, here was this boy, rather wayward—
rather inclined to " moon," his father may have put
it—perturbed, as he tells us, by the feeling that he
was " somehow different " from others, and not
knowing whether that difference boded him good
or ill, with no fixed idea, no definite plan as to what
he was going to do in life. The problem is not an
unfamiliar one. It has frequently presented itself
to parents in narrow circumstances who have
managed somehow or another to send their boy as a
day scholar to some public school, but have not the

means to let him complete his studies at the University. He tells us that Law, Medicine, the Army and the Civil Service all presented themselves as possible careers, but that he rejected them, either because he had no taste for them or because he considered himself devoid of the special capabilities that would have enabled him to pursue them with any reasonable prospect of success. It may have been that these considerations were reinforced by a sense of the sacrifice that " bringing him to a profession " would entail on his parents. If so he— and the rest of the world—have indeed reason to be grateful to Poverty, the beneficent mother who dedicated his days to the service of Art and Beauty. " She preserved me from folly," he says. What is at least as important is that she preserved him from mere professional eminence, possibly—since his heart would have been otherwhere—from professional mediocrity. There was, of course, commerce—business. That occurred to him, not, if we are to take him literally, because it would be immediately productive and needed no lengthy apprenticeship, but because he had read in some English eighteenth-century romances of certain merchants who cut a goodish figure with their coats of crimson or maroon cloth and their warehouses filled with bales of merchandise. It would have been as though some nursling of the Muses were to be lured to an office in Mincing Lane because he had

> Descried at sunrise an emerging prow
> Lifting the cool hair'd creepers stealthily,
> The fringes of a Southward-facing brow
> Among the Ægean isles;
> And saw the merry Grecian coaster come,
> Freighted with amber grapes, and Chian wine,
> Green bursting figs, and tunnies steep'd in brine—

Fathers are sometimes apt to be apathetic, slipshod even, in these circumstances, and the " père France," surrounded by his cronies who haunted the shop on the Quai Voltaire, his head filled with his Catholic and Royalist enthusiasms, may not have thought over much about his son's future. That, too, was as well, for he might have put his paternal foot down with possibly disastrous results to the literature of our age. One of the boy's school friends suggested agriculture, but, though he confesses that the day was to come when the country would be his only love and that he was fated to pass there the happiest and pleasantest years of his life, he could not then bring himself to bid adieu, with no prospect of returning, to the City " where Art and Beauty flourish and the very stones seem to sing." " Moreover," he adds, " I had a good reason for not farming my land : I had no land to farm." And so he just drifted, we may almost say he " loafed "; but always we may be sure, under the vigilant yet indulgent eye of his mother. *She* knew he was a genius and she possessed a faculty that, perhaps fortunately, is not commonly granted to the mothers of ordinary folk : her keen olfactory sense generally enabled her to discover "what company the beings whom she loved had been keeping when out of her sight." He loafed then, but how profitably ! There were the conversations in his father's shop, of which we have a model in the logomachies between his godfather Monsieur Danquin, who worshipped Napoleon, and Monsieur Dubois, who despised him. There were the Galleries and the Museums. To reach the Louvre he had but to cross the Seine and thither he went almost daily, " So that I may say with truth, that my youth was nurtured amid the splendours of a palace."

The really valuable part of a University training resides perhaps less in the lectures and courses of study followed there than in the intercourse with others, in the clash of ideas, and in the influence wrought upon the spirit by the scenes, the material setting, of a place devoted for centuries to the pursuit of learning. For Monsieur France, to whom a regular university career was denied, Paris, especially the " Borough side " of Paris, as Lamb called the *rive gauche*, was his Alma Mater, the Latin Quarter, his common-room. " Ye old rapacious Jews of the Rue du Cherche Midi," he exclaims, " ye artless book vendors of the quays, my masters all ! How greatly am I beholden to you ! To you I owe as much, nay even more than to school itself, for the training of my intellect. It was you, good folk, who displayed to my enchanted gaze the mysterious tokens of a bygone age and all manner of precious memorials of the pilgrimage of the human mind. Even as I turned over the old tomes in your boxes, or gazed within your dusty stalls laden with the sad relics of our sires and their golden thoughts, I became insensibly imbued with the most wholesome of philosophies. Yes, my friends, it was when rummaging about among those musty books, those scraps of tarnished metal-work, those fragments of old, worm-eaten carvings which you used to barter for your daily bread, that my childish spirit recognized how frail and fleeting are all the things of this world. I divined that we living beings were but ever-changing figures in the world's great Shadow Show; and even then my heart inclined to sadness, gentleness and pity."

All this was well, supremely well, and we at this date know the rich fruit that this apprenticeship was to bear. But applying Anatole France's own method of viewing history to the particular stage in his career at which he had now arrived, we may wonder whether " père France " was quite satisfied at the progress his son was making towards achieving a position that would enable him to earn his daily bread. There were " dreams to sell " and in abundance, but dreams are, at the best, not very readily marketable, and not at all so when they are still imprisoned in the head of the dreamer. Fortunately the elder France was not a very practical man and, commercially speaking, not a very successful one, or the boy's dreams might not have been so uninterrupted or his loafing so prolonged.

CHAPTER III

THE *ÉDUCATION SENTIMENTALE*

HEN he passed his *baccalauréat*, Anatole France would have been about sixteen or seventeen, and from seventeen to the early twenties is a critical period for a young man. " As a child I had shown great intelligence," he tells us, " but when I was about seventeen I grew stupid. I used to be so nervous in those days that I could not make my bow or take my seat in company without my forehead becoming moist with perspiration. The presence of women sent me off into a panic."

In the work of Monsieur France there is a considerable quantity of what the classical commentators term internal evidence tending to show that he succeeded in overcoming this fatal weakness, a weakness which, in a recent essay, he notes—doubtless with the compassion natural to a fellow-sufferer— as having at one time afflicted Stendhal, who also appears to have vanquished it pretty completely.

At the age of seventeen, however, there is no

doubt that he was bashful to the point of morbidity. On one occasion—he tells the story at length in *My Friend's Book*—he was so overcome by timidity that he said " Yes, sir," as he might have done to one of his schoolmasters, when a lady, beautiful but many years his senior, asked him, after playing a Nocturne of Chopin's, whether he cared for music. His agony of mind was great—" Those two words, ' Yes, sir,' were for ever ringing in my ears," he writes. " The recollection of them was always with me, or, to speak more accurately, some horrible psychical phenomenon made it seem as though time had suddenly come to a standstill, and that the dreadful moment that had been startled by that irreparable utterance, ' Yes, sir,' was being indefinitely prolonged. . . . For six weeks I remained in a condition of sombre melancholy. . . ." It was unnecessary. He had merely offered convincing proof that the lady's charm had caused him to lose his head, and what greater compliment than that could a woman desire.

He was in love ; but he did not know it. It was not till six months later when he was spending his holiday at a little village in Normandy—where he beheld the sea for the first time—that the nature of his malady was revealed to him. And the revelation was brought about by a poet. It was the *Hic quos durus amor* . . . of Virgil that opened his eyes.

" Here," sings the greatest of Roman poets, " here shy glades conceal those whom unrelenting love hath with cruel venom consumed in lingering death and all around them groves of myrtle cast their shade."

" Oh, I knew it ! I knew that grove of myrtle. But I knew not its name. Virgil had now revealed it to me. I knew that it was love."

All this took place when he was still at school ; he had just finished—and with credit—his course of rhetoric, which is about equivalent to the fifth form in an English school. But considerably later on we find him saying, " My fondness for women was far too excessive to be displayed, and it made me coy and timid in their society." It was a state of mind fraught with great possibilities, possibilities which in his case were fully realized ; for we have but to read the *Rôtisserie de la Reine Pédauque* to appreciate that his acquaintance with woman was no mere Platonic matter.

When, for example, the Abbé Jérôme Coignard says, " Look at this pretty girl . . . her little head, her beautiful throat, her charmingly rounded form and all the rest. In what corner of her person could a grain of virtue find lodgment ? There is no room, all is so firm, so full of sap, plump and well filled. Virtue, like the raven, lives among the ruins. It is to be found in the lines and wrinkles of the body," he is clearly speaking *en connaissance de cause*, and implying a theory of virtue that has perhaps a good deal to be said for it.

Woman as a beautiful animal, the lure of physical love, these manifestly became familiar to him, and if in his own case he tastes of them with moderation, it is because, with fine Epicurean wisdom, he is anxious to avoid the drab horror of satiety; because he is fain to retain " the only real boon there is in this life, the boon which imbues with loveliness and grace the beings and the things we care for, which sheds over the world its perfume and its charm, the boon of Desire." But this is to anticipate. Long after the incident recorded above we find him awkward and shy in the presence of women, but overwhelmingly impressed by their charm. When, a schoolboy no longer but a young man, he is introduced to a beautiful Russian woman at a friend's house, he loses all his composure. " In a moment I had lost the use of my senses; all my faculties deserted me, my self-possession, my reason even. . . . Her voice fell on my ears like a caress and gave me a delicious sense of pain. It was a strange voice, a little barbaric in tone, and it was a voice that sang. I do not know how long I remained there bereft of the power of speech; " and then he adds, " I had penetrated the secret of Eros. I had learned that pure love emancipates itself from all such things as sympathy, regard, affection. It lives upon desire and feeds upon illusion. I had all that one may hope to win from love : a phantom."

Be that as it may, it is quite certain that Anatole France, who relishes a *gauloiserie*, a " merry tale," as thoroughly as Rabelais or Sterne, who can be of the earth earthy, who can be as coarse, if you will, as Shakespeare or Defoe, was not always content with these unincarnate attachments. But the Mesdames de Bonmont, de Gromance, des Aubels and the rest were later experiences. For the present he was the shy, unsophisticated boy whose serenity was grievously troubled by this vague mysterious longing called Love, which had not yet materialized into *volupté*. How and when did he serve his apprenticeship in the Art of Love ? How and when did he come by the key that opens the portals of Life and Death ? For Love, the physical love of a man for a woman, is but the expression of that nostalgy, that home-sickness which lures him thither whence he came, to drain the " darker drink " of oblivion. For he who seeks out Volupté to linger in her arms, though he scatters the seeds of life, for himself, in the end, reaps only Death ; the joy of it is the joy *de se perdre*. None knows better than Anatole France this eternal commingling of Joy and Sorrow, Love and Death. But this was a wisdom that was to come later.

E

Meantime he continued his *flâneries* and was to
continue them for a long time to come. The idea
of entering on a mercantile career he had set aside,
baffled by the difficulty of selecting which particular
branch of commerce he should undertake, for,
glancing through the Directory which gave a list
of the various trades in their alphabetical order, he
discovered that he was equally apt or inapt for them
all. But all this while he felt the desire to write
stirring within him. Yet he was in no haste to set
pen to paper. He did not fall a victim to that fatal
precocity that too often assails the youthful aspirant
to literary fame. The probability is that Anatole
France was not ambitious in the ordinary sense.
The true visionary rarely is : he is too much wrapt
up in his dreams. Certainly he was too deeply
imbued with reverence for Form, too completely
possessed with admiration for those classic masterpieces, " the birth of some chance morning or
evening at an Ionian festival or among the Sabine
Hills, which have lasted for thousands of years with
a power over the mind and a charm which the current
literature of our day with all its obvious advantages
is utterly unable to rival," to hanker after a facile
literary success. And he knew how frail and
transitory a thing is literary renown and how few
of those innumerable writers who had a vogue in
their day have withstood the corrosion of time.

" For my part," he says, " I have never lighted upon an original edition of Molière or Racine on the Quays ; but I have gathered there something of even greater worth . . . I have found wisdom there. All those piles of paper begrimed with printer's ink have taught me the vanity of triumphs that fade, of glory which blossoms but to die. Never do I turn over the contents of the penny box but a calm and gentle melancholy steals into my heart and I say : ' what avails it to add yet a few more pages to this mass of ink-stained paper ? Surely it were better to write no more.' " Yet he did write. But because he was able to bide his time, because he wrote to please himself, and not to catch the public ear, he has so written that some at least of his work will endure as long as the taste for literature survives in the human mind.

Thus, for some long time yet, he was, as he tells us, to live happy years, writing nothing, leading a solitary and contemplative life. The only distraction that beguiled this lonely existence, which saw the dreaming child grow into the meditative youth, were his daily visits to the book stalls wherein his early masters displayed their dusty wares to those who came and went along the Quays of the Seine. Notwithstanding that he looked to make no startling discovery among these weather-beaten volumes—the days when one might hope to fish

an Aldine or an Elzevir out of the twopenny box
had now long since gone by—he took the purest
delight in searching these stalls and in holding
friendly converse with their proprietors. " I shall,"
he says, " always remember with delight the long
hours I have spent at their stalls with the friendly
skies above me, now iridescent with countless
delicate tints, now glorious in hues of purple and
gold, now clad in silver grey, but grey of such
witching softness that the deeps of the heart were
touched by it. When all is said and done, I know
of no sweeter, gentler pleasure than to go a book-
hunting along the Quays of Paris. As you stir up
the dust of the penny box you wake from their
slumbers countless ghosts of tragic or alluring aspect.
From these lonely abodes you may evoke the spirits
of the departed as with an enchanter's wand. You
may hold converse with the dead who come in
throngs in answer to your summons. For all the
praise the ancients bestowed on them, the Elysian
Fields could offer nothing to a dead philosopher
that a live Parisian cannot enjoy on the Quays here
between the Pont Royal and the Pont Notre-Dame."
There, then, for a time we may leave him.

CHAPTER IV

THE LITERARY DEBUT

ABOUT fifty years ago, a group of young men were in the habit of meeting, one evening a week, at a certain house in the Rue de Condé, where they would talk about literature in general, and poetry in particular. The house afforded an appropriate *milieu* for these literary gatherings, for it had formerly belonged to no less a personage than Caron de Beaumarchais, the author of *Le Mariage de Figaro* and—as is currently held—the unwitting instigator of the French Revolution. The house, modest enough in size, was full of things that recalled the memory of the illustrious writer. Paintings representing scenes from classical mythology still adorned the walls of the bath-room and the principal bedroom, and from ground floor to attic, everything about the dwelling was eloquent of the days of Louis XV.

This historic abode had become the property of Monsieur Bonnières de Wières, who had handed on the usufruct of it to his son, Monsieur Robert de

Bonnières. The latter counted among his many friends Coquelin Cadet, Père Dulong de Rosnay, Monsieur Munier and Anatole France. On a table in a corner of the *salon* where the meetings took place, stood a small cask of beer festooned with branches of fir. At this cask, which was fitted with a boxwood tap, any member of the company was free to assuage his thirst. Here a deal of talk went on, diversified by song, and Coquelin perhaps would recite a monologue from his inexhaustible réper-toire. At midnight the party would disperse, after arranging for their next meeting, and the street, deserted at this hour, would echo to the footsteps of the departing members of this informal but enthusiastic *cénacle*.

Though there was noise in plenty at these gather-ings, an abundance of mirth and laughter, not one of these young men but was a worker, not excepting the richest among them; and Anatole France, a bookseller's son and reared in an atmosphere of books, had determined to be a writer. He had dreamed of it in his school days; now his mind was made up. He was doubtless encouraged in his literary aspirations by his friends, and, not least among them, by Monsieur Robert de Bonnières, who himself became a writer of note and who has be-queathed us a valuable portrait of Anatole France as he was at this date. " Never have I known a man," says Monsieur de Bonnières, " less fitted for action than Anatole France; never have I known a man with a greater gift for the regular exercise of his intellectual faculties, or one endowed with so marked a disposition to grasp things and to understand them. Thus his friends found in him a good and useful counsellor. His constitutional unselfishness was portrayed upon his long and placid features, in his rather dreamy physiognomy, and in the languor of his expression, which was kindly, visionary and gentle; it was even evident in his mode of speech, which was hesitating and embarrassed."

It was not only in the house of Monsieur de Bonnières that Anatole France forgathered with his friends. His home being close to the Luxembourg, thither he would betake himself on warm sunny mornings with a group of friends. Bourget would hold forth with eloquence on the philosophy of criticism, Frédéric Plessis—an elegant scholar and afterwards *Maître de Conférences* at Poitiers—would read verses agreeably classical in tone and sentiment, Camille Benoit, who was later to write an overture and incidental music for *Les Noces Corinthiennes*, would expound the genius and art of Berlioz, beneath the shade of the plane trees. Their main topics were Science, Science in all its branches, and Love; and they dwelled together in peace.

There have been preserved to us some interesting vignettes, or thumb-nail sketches, which Anatole France jotted down for his own amusement and for the entertainment of his friends concerning some of his poetic contemporaries. They are couched in the succinct, staccato style of entries in a diary:

" Sully Prudhomme. 36. Former student of the École Polytechnique. Has remained mathematical and geometrical even in his sonnets. Given to love-making and algebra. Solves problems of passion by means of equations. Intellectual and profound, but losing his bloom. Has suffered from ill-health. Rich and handsome. Finds life a bore.

" Paul Bourget. Son of an illustrious mathematician. Fashionable Normalien (student of the École Normale). A lover, of the intellectual type. The most perfect product of the Quartier Latin. A living refutation of the absurd legend created by Murger. Very young and very learned. An admirer of Spinoza.

" Heredia. 32. Handsome, rich. A Spanish grandee. High-sounding and heroic. Writes better verses than Hugo.

" Armand Silvestre. An angelic Priapus. Has only had one thing to say. Up to now he has never said it but always hovered round about it. Neither men, women, nor scenery in his verse. A spasm.

Bears too close a resemblance to women; at once sentimental and hysterical.

" Frédéric Plessis. Much talent. Sentimental and an artist.

" Cazalis. Formerly Cazelli. 35. Talent; grace, intelligence. A dandified sceptic. A drawing-room Darwinian. Very much in love with the East—a somewhat Café Anglais East. Has one fault: he is fond of women poets and women painters.

" André Lemagne. Young; very young; excessively young. Has been young for 35 years. Little, but perfect. A one-small-book man, like the author of the *Imitation*. The only poet in the world who doesn't write about choice flowers. He can tell any sort of tree from the smallest piece of bark."

Of the above, the first three, Sully Prudhomme, Paul Bourget and Jose Maria de Heredia, all preceded Anatole France into the Academy. Paul Bourget was the only one among them who forsook the poetic Muse and attained distinction as a prose writer.

The earliest recorded " work " of Anatole France is *The Legend of Saint Radegonde*, a schoolboy exercise which he dedicated to " un père et une mère bien aimés " and which a proud uncle caused to be lithographed. The story of the beautiful and

virtuous Thuringian princess, which he had doubtless
first learned at his mother's knee, is related with becoming piety ; it is interesting because, at least in its
dedication, it conveys some hint—which his study
of Alfred de Vigny scarcely does—of the rhythm
and cadence, of those characteristic turns of phrase,
which were destined to mark his style in its maturity.

"Dear parents," he says, " the first words which
the child utters on earth are *maman, papa !* They
are the only words he knows, and so he applies
them to all things : if he is ill, he cries ' Maman ' ;
if he desires anything, he says ' Maman ' ; if he
needs help, he calls ' Maman ' ; then, when his
mother has taught him to express certain ideas,
he says, ' Maman, I love you ; papa, I love you.'
These words, which are a hymn of gratitude,
prompted neither by fear nor by cupidity, are the
expression of a perfectly natural affection. Thus
it is with all children, thus it is with your Anatole.
And now when, thanks to your care of him, he is
learning to use words as men use them, he will not
show less gratitude than the little child that expresses its love for its mother with such simplicity
and truth. He will dedicate to you every line
that comes from his pen. On every page he writes
you may read ' To my dear parents.' Moreover,
to what judges more indulgent or more favourably
disposed could I present my feeble efforts ? Your

devoted son : Anatole France Thibault, 20th November, 1859."

In this effusion the note of self-complacency, which is the almost inevitable characteristic of *juvenilia*, is obviously not lacking, but, here and there, is a hint, faint indeed, but unmistakable, of the incomparable music to come.

Anatole France was not a precocious writer. He was not one of those who, like a Macaulay or a Bryce, will produce, when they are scarcely out of their teens, work bearing upon it all the characteristics of maturity. His Minerva, most emphatically, " was not born in panoply." But when he says, " j'ai vécu d'heureuses années sans écrire " we must not take the statement too literally. From 1867, at all events, he did not let a year go by without sending something to the press. His friend Étienne Charavay, a scholar and a charming companion, initiated him into the science of manuscripts, and France served a profitable apprenticeship at the École des Chartes. Charavay was the inaugurator of the systematic study of autographs and, under his encouragement, Anatole France contributed fairly frequently to the *Amateur d'autographes*. He also wrote with some degree of regularity for the *Chasseur bibliographique*, the *Gazette bibliographique*, the *Bibliophile français* and the *Gazette rimée*. It was thus that he served his apprenticeship to the "métier." In the *Chasseur bibliographique*, Monsieur France played a double rôle, or rather a treble one. He was its sub-editor, and he reviewed books under the name, A. Thibault, and plays under that of Anatole France. Besides all this, there were the "Préfaces" to certain editions of French classics, "Éditions de bibliophile," which he wrote at the behest of the publisher Lemerre. Later on he gathered the most important of them together in a single volume under the title of *Le Génie Latin* dedicated "très affectueusement" to Désiré Lemerre. Some at least of these "Préfaces" must have revealed to such as read them—and they were probably few enough—that a writer of some achievement and no ordinary promise had dawned upon the literary horizon. The collected edition, published in January 1913, contains the following prefatory note:

"Found no lofty expectations on this title, *The Latin Genius* ; you will find here nothing to justify them. It is an act of faith and of love for that Greek and Latin tradition wherein resides all wisdom and beauty, and without whose pale is naught but error and vexation of spirit. Philosophy, Art, Science, Jurisprudence, all, we owe to Greece and to her conquerors whom she overcame. The men of old time live on and teach us yet."

These essays are of the true vintage; they are
authentic France, albeit a little harsh and crude
at times. They differ in finish only, not in substance, from some of the best examples of *La Vie
Littéraire*. The essay on Chateaubriand which,
with that on Bernardin de Saint-Pierre, is perhaps
the best thing in the collection, has very much in
it to arrest the attention. First of all we find the
campi lugentes still haunting him. Those myrtle
shades of which Virgil sings in lines which had
brought to him as a youth so deep a revelation,
still cast their spell upon him. He pictures
Chateaubriand " stretched on the grass, or in his
boat, book in hand . . . he could see the heroines
of poetry and romance; particularly could he see
Tibullus's Delia, the sinner of Massilon's sermon,
and the immortal and glowing form who, from
among the Virgilian myrtles, exercises her enchantments across the ages on the chosen youth of each
generation." Thus he writes of Chateaubriand,
but it is of himself that he is thinking, and he
cannot forbear from the pleasure of transcribing
the whole passage in which the Phœnician Queen
is depicted as wandering in the shadows of a deep
wood, dimly seen in the gloom, even as a man
descries, or thinks he descries, the sickle moon
rising amid the clouds. " Happy," he cries,
" happy are they who thrill to that miracle of

poetry. The world knows, perhaps, a thousand such lines. Were they to perish, earth would be less fair." There, then, is the poet-critic, and critics of this type are, like the poets themselves, born, not made. Happy, indeed, are they who thrill to that miracle of poetry. But who, save the gods, shall impart the gift? This passage engraved itself deep on his imagination. Later on, in a story comprised in the collection entitled *Mother of Pearl*, the hero of the tale says "up to that time I had known nothing of women, except Lavinia in the *Æneid* and Mademoiselle Rose. Then I realized Dido, and flames seemed to rush through my veins. The image of the unhappy Queen, who, tortured by an irremediable wound, wandered in the forest of myrtles, bent at night over my troubled couch. Moreover, if I walked out in the evening, I seemed to be aware of her dead white figure gliding between the bushes in the woods, as the moon passes through the midst of the clouds."

Allusions to this passage may be found *passim* throughout his work. In *The Bloom of Life*, for instance, he tells how, when midway through his school career, he was called upon to choose whether he would "read" Classics or Science; he decided to "opt" for Science. "For three days," he goes on, "I held firmly to my resolve, but on the

fourth the Virgilian myrtles and the hidden path-
way of the forest of shades renewed their old
temptation."

Later on in the same essay on Chateaubriand,
there is another quotation, or rather allusion,
which is of singular interest, particularly to English
readers; it is a reference to the opening lines of
Act I, Scene VI of *Macbeth*.   Duncan, with his
retinue of chieftains, is approaching Macbeth's
castle.   The lines assigned by Shakespeare to the
doomed King are as follows :

> This castle hath a pleasant seat; the air
> Nimbly and sweetly recommends itself
> Unto our gentle senses.

And then Banquo comments thus :

> This guest of summer,
> The temple haunting martlet, does approve
> By his loved mansionry that the heaven's breath
> Smells wooingly here : no jutty, frieze,
> Buttress, nor coign of vantage, but this bird
> Hath made his pendent bed and procreant cradle :
> Where they most breed and haunt, I have observed
> The air is delicate.

It is, of course, a passage of great beauty, but not
one, perhaps, that we should naturally expect to
impress itself upon a foreign reader.   It has not
the obvious rhetorical force of many other passages
in the same play, passages one would have thought
far better calculated to excite the admiration of
a reader steeped in Racine.   Yet when he describes

the towers and turrets of the ancestral home of
the Chateaubriands, it is the castle of Macbeth
that "creeps into his study of imagination."
"Martins," says Duncan the King, "breed only
where the air is delicate, and, in summer, the
martins sought the crevices of Combourg's walls."
Only the words were Banquo's and not Duncan's.

Of *Macbeth* and of *Hamlet* he seems indeed to
have made an especially careful study. He speaks
in the course of his essay on *Hamlet at the Comédie
Française*, of "the blood of a fatherly old king
staining the *little* hands of Lady Macbeth," and
his remembering that wonderful adjective, without
which we might have forgotten, in our horror at
the crime, that Lady Macbeth was, after all, a
woman and a beautiful woman, proves him of the
true poetic lineage. That *little* hand—how ordinary
yet how tremendous the epithet—stands out white
and delicate and eternally pathetic against the
dark and terrible background of the play, turning
our horror into pity.

In 1868 there appeared, with the imprint of
Bachelin-Deflorenne, who carried on the business
of a bookseller and publisher at No. 3 Quai Malaquais, a modest little volume, consisting of some
hundred and fifty beautifully printed pages, devoted
to Alfred de Vigny. It was adorned with an
etching of Vigny by G. Staal, and its author was

Anatole France. The book was one of a series of " études," to which various writers contributed, designed to appeal to the bibliophile. " This little book," says its author, " has not been written to pander to the curiosity of the idle or inquisitive." He has essayed, he goes on to observe, to tell the plain story of a great poet and an upright man, because it seemed to him instructive to discover the conditions amid which great works are produced and the soil upon which the austere flowers of the mind unfold their petals. Poetry, he continues, is not merely a game in which success may be achieved by skilful arrangement and a sort of sleight of hand. It is not met with apart from self-respect and elevation of ideas. " My aim," he says in conclusion, " has been to display the exemplar of a beautiful life, which gave beautiful work to the world."

Anatole France had long nourished an admiration for the singer who, in Mill's phrase, " chaunts from the poem of human life, in a voice of subdued sadness, a few strains telling of obscure wisdom and unrewarded virtue ; of those antique characters, which, without self-glorification or hope of being appreciated, ' carry out ' the sentiment of duty to its extremest consequences." As a youth, Monsieur France tells us in *The Bloom of Life*, it had seemed to him a splendid thing to be an officer, granted,

F

of course, he was of the type portrayed by Alfred de Vigny, melancholy and magnanimous. "I had devoured," he says, "with passionate eagerness *Servitude et Grandeur Militaires.*" Whether it was that his admiration for the Romantics was beginning to wane—it is in this book that he speaks of the din that went on in Victor Hugo's head drowning the whispered messages of the Past—or whether some restrictions as to the treatment of his subject had been laid upon him, it is generally admitted that this little book contains no hint, or scarcely any, of those qualities which were to make him the foremost man of letters of his generation.

It was when he had been working for some time for Lemerre, at whose establishment the Parnassians used to hold their enthusiastic and generally tumultuous gatherings, that Anatole France obtained a position in the Library of the Senate.

One would naturally imagine that a young man who, in his earlier days, had regarded with unqualified envy a certain Père Le Beau (of whom we read in *My Friend's Book*) because he spent his days and nights compiling catalogues, inscribing the names and descriptions of books on endless pieces of cardboard, would have found here an employment admirably suited to his taste; for what happier destiny could one conceive for a man of letters than to pass his days in the studious calm

of some stately library, where innumerable volumes
hold in their keeping the wisdom of the ages, where
spacious windows offer to the eye, when weary
with poring too diligently upon the printed page,
the restful and refreshing prospect of trim gardens
and graceful statuary ? Such an abode of dignified
learning is the Library of the Senate in Paris which,
as everybody knows, is housed in the Palais du
Luxembourg.   Here, in the early seventies,
dwelled together three poets whose names were
Lacaussade, Ratisbonne and Leconte de Lisle.
Candid and innocent minds would doubtless picture
these three singers as passing their days together in
utter harmony.   Alas, if the melancholy truth must
be told, the intercourse of poets upon earth is not
generally marked by that amity and concord which
prevails among them when

In solemn troops and sweet societies,

they meet and converse together in the glades and
groves of Elysium.   The fact is that, before they
have shuffled off this mortal coil, they are too often
a prey to those jealousies and bickerings by which
ordinary humanity is commonly afflicted.   Of this
truth, the three poets of the Luxembourg offered
only too striking an example.   Though they were
colleagues, theirs was not a brotherhood of song.
To be quite frank, they hated each other like poison.

Lacaussade and Ratisbonne, though but mediocre poets, were above Leconte de Lisle in the official hierarchy. As may be imagined, the situation was not precisely calculated to make for peace. Lacaussade was a dapper, rather dandified little person, with a most official mind. He was so *administratif* or, as we should say, so much in love with red tape, that he came to be nicknamed " le parfait notaire de la poésie." Against Leconte de Lisle he had developed a special animus. He accused him of having made away with one of the books in the Library because it contained a reference to the pension granted him by Napoleon III out of his privy purse. When he brought this charge, Lacaussade was, it would seem, conveniently oblivious of the fact that he himself had been in the pay of the *Revue européenne*, an organ subsidized by the Empire. The author of *Poèmes Barbares* replied with vigour, and Lacaussade spoke bitterly of the ingratitude of the man who had once been so friendly with him as to borrow his collars and— his pants! How Leconte de Lisle, who was a well-set-up man, contrived to get them on is a mystery of which Lacaussade in his indignation offers no elucidation. Leconte de Lisle replied by lampooning his colleague in verses in which he called him " Coco " and " Zanzibar," appellations apparently designed to convey the unflattering suggestion of a none too remote simian ancestry. Lacaussade retorted that Leconte de Lisle was like a looking-glass that only reflected the objects shown in it; that he was a swollen sponge; a gaudy dahlia without scent, and, finally, a pompous nincompoop, a whey-faced clown.

As for Ratisbonne, the third member of this poetic trio, he was apparently the most cantankerous of the three. He was a protégé of Monsieur Thiers, and he used to give out with pride that he had been given his appointment *à titre de récompense nationale.* So strained were the relations between Ratisbonne and Lacaussade that on one occasion — *tantæne animis cœlestibus iræ !* — they fought a duel—with umbrellas—at the entrance to the Palais. Matters could not continue like this, and a sort of peace was patched up between the combatants. It must have been little more than an armed neutrality, since the most cordial view that Lacaussade could bring himself to express concerning his confrère was that he was not so much a knave as a fool—" Ce n'est pas un méchant homme que Ratisbonne, mais c'est un sot."

Before we take leave of this refractory trinity—of whom we may well ask *quis custodiet ipsos custodes?*—one little fact concerning Leconte de Lisle is worth recording, since it shows that, notwithstanding the classic dignity of his Muse, he believed, like Horace, that it is a salutary thing to play the fool in the proper place. It appears that for a period of a few years the Senate Library was thrown open to the public. This concession to the *profanum vulgus* was strongly resented by Leconte de Lisle, and he invented an ingenious method of baffling any member of the public who should be so rash as to avail himself of the permission to invade the sacred precincts. Round the whole extent of the Library runs a corridor, from which, at intervals, little passages give access to the Library itself. Leconte de Lisle caused to be stuck up along the walls of this corridor placards bearing an arrow pointing straight ahead, with the legend " to the library " ; so that a stranger would sometimes circumambulate the corridor surrounding the library two or three times, only to find himself back again at the point whence he had started.

Into this genial company, about the year 1874, came Anatole France, who appears to have owed his nomination to Leconte de Lisle and Lacaussade. As we have seen, his study of Alfred de Vigny had attracted some attention, as had also the prefaces which Lemerre had commissioned him to write. The emoluments accruing from this source were not on a princely scale. They seem, indeed, to have been modest to the point of exiguity. Literary work of this kind affords a welcome addition to one's revenue. It scarcely provides a livelihood. For this reason—but not, as will appear, for this reason alone—his friends, the librarian and the sub-librarian, invited the promising young essayist to join the Library staff. He came, under the not very imposing title of *commis surveillant*. In addition to his salary, he had an *appartement* and an allowance of wood, coal and oil. But it swiftly became apparent that he was to do his own work and that of his three seniors, who, though at loggerheads on most matters, were unanimous on that. Lacaussade, who had instituted what he called "le service extérieur de la bibliothèque," persuading the authorities to confirm the innovation, was rarely at his post. He used to leave a note on his desk saying that he had gone to the Beaux Arts, or some such place, on Library business, and that he would not be back any more that day. Ratisbonne, whose sole duty was to enter up the new books in a register, found even this task onerous, and unworthy of so gifted a man. "Couldn't they do without buying all these books?" he exclaimed. "They serve no useful purpose." Sound sense enough, perhaps, but surely most unlibrarian-like. The Senators complained of the inefficiency of the Library staff. The superintendent, Charles Edmond, the novelist, more famous for the majesty of his beard than for the

quality of his fiction, " came down " on Lacaussade,
Ratisbonne and Leconte de Lisle; they, in turn,
put the screw on Anatole France. Anatole France
was far from docile. He had his rooms taken away
from him on the not unreasonable grounds that he
never used them. He was ordered to compile an
elaborate catalogue. In an ironic letter, he asked
for authority to visit, at the public expense, the
various Libraries of Europe, with a view to dis-
covering the best method of compiling a catalogue.
The situation became daily more strained, and
in no long time France resigned his post.

But there had been an interlude to these literary
occupations. When the war of 1870 broke out,
the pen was exchanged for the sword. Anatole
France became a soldier, and he tells us how,
during the battle of the 2nd December, being
among the troops held in reserve beneath the fort
of the Faisanderie, he read through the *Silenus* of
Virgil, amid the noise of the shells that dropped
in front of him in the waters of the Marne. The
picture recalls Chateaubriand reading his Homer
beneath the walls of Thionville.

Enamoured as he was of the eighteenth century
and all its works, Monsieur France, whatever views
he may hold to-day, has not always been inspired
by pacificist ideals. " The military virtues," he
wrote in *Le Temps* many years ago, " The military

virtues! Why, they are responsible for the whole of civilization. Industry, the arts, police, they gave birth to them all. . . . These beneficent warriors laid the foundations of the fatherland and the State; they made secure the safety of the commonwealth; they promoted the arts and industries of peace, which it had been impossible to carry on before them. They gave birth, little by little, to all those great sentiments which still form the basis of the State to-day; for together with the city, they founded the spirit of order, of devotion, of sacrifice, of obedience to the laws and of love of their fellow-countrymen. Such was the work wrought by the army when it was but made up of a band of half-naked savages. Since then it has been the most powerful agent of civilization and progress. The sword has always given power to those most worthy to wield it. People complain that the army stands for force and nothing but force. But let us remember that this same force took the place of anarchy, and that wherever a regular army has been lacking, domestic massacres have been of daily occurrence. The soldier is necessary, and of all things which the fates have entailed upon society, the most constant and the most imperious is war.

"I will go so far as to say that war is humane, in that it is proper to the human race. It regulates

violence and thus constitutes the greatest result
that the human race has hitherto obtained from
the process of civilization.   Shall we do still better
some day?   Shall war cease and the soldier disappear?   Such hopes are chimerical and it is
dangerous to work for their fulfilment.

" Man cannot evade the ordinances of his origin.
It is his nature to be violent.   When he becomes
pacific, he will no longer be man but some unknown
being of which we have not even a presentiment.
Shall I out with it?   The more I think of it, the
less I dare to hope that war will cease.   I should
be afraid lest, if it disappeared, this great and
terrible power should bear away with it the virtues
to which it gave rise and which still form the basis
of our social edifice to-day.   Do away with military
virtues and the whole fabric of society will fall
about our ears."

These sentiments sounded strangely from the
Tower of Ivory.   One might have justly entertained the hypothesis that the gentle flute player,
its original occupant, had been evicted by some
truculent apostle of the gospel of blood and iron.
It is at all events a skilful little apologia for the
Army and *les vertus militaires* and furnishes salutary
doctrine for those visionary politicians who seem to
hold that the nature of man, who is a fearful and
therefore a ferocious animal, is to be changed in

the twinkling of an eye. This essay which originally appeared in *Le Temps* was subsequently incorporated, in part, in a preface written by Monsieur France to Camille Benoit's translation of Goethe's *Faust*, published by Lemerre in 1891. Fortunately the human memory is short or the future determined opponent of the three years' military service act might have been somewhat nonplussed if these earlier words of his had been quoted against him. They are indeed in striking contrast to the sentiments expressed to Jacques Tournebroche by the Abbé Jérôme Coignard in Chapter X of his *Opinions*. " I have worked," said he, " at all trades save that of a soldier, which has always filled me with disgust and terror, by the characteristics of servitude, false glory, and cruelty attached to it. . . . And I own to you, my son, that military service seems to me the most terrible pest of civilized nations. . . . Men must needs be light and frivolous, my son, to give more honour to a soldier's doings than to the work of a farm-labourer and to place the havoc of war at a higher price than the arts of peace."

CHAPTER V

THE PARNASSIANS

LEMERRE carried on his business of publisher and bookseller at No. 23 Passage du Choiseul, and there it was, as we have said, that the Parnassians used to meet and hold their debates, if indeed one may describe these tumultuous logomachies by so sedate a term. The fact is that, like Gil Blas and the adversaries whom he engaged in argument, these disputants might have been taken for people possessed of a devil rather than for philosophers or poets. The room in which the Parnassians forgathered was situated directly above Lemerre's shop, with which it communicated by a spiral staircase. As there was no chairman or any sort of presidential control to check the forensic exuberance of the speakers, there was nothing to hinder them from all speaking at once—a freedom of which they liberally availed themselves. So alarming did the uproar occasionally become, that intending purchasers about to visit the shop below would—if they did not incontinently bolt—pause in timorous hesitation on the threshold until they were reassured by Lemerre's factotum, who blandly explained that there was no cause for alarm, and added confidentially that it was " only the poets upstairs discussing æsthetics." Whenever the din overhead became unbearable, Lemerre would ascend the spiral staircase and gaze about him with an expression of dignified reproach, like Father Neptune surveying the rebellious waters. The effect was instantaneous. Hardly had his head, with its fine tawny beard, emerged above the level of the floor than a sudden hush fell upon the assembly. Their breasts were soothed, harmony was restored—for a while.

When, in the late sixties, France made his appearance among this company, he was looked at not a little askance by some of its members. It was, perhaps, held by certain of the more revolutionary among them that the son of the ex-guardsman of Charles X was bound to be imbued with his father's Catholic and Royalist principles. In point of fact nothing could have been wider of the truth. We know, on his own confession, how widely he differed both in temperament and opinion from his father. His culture was already too wide and varied, his understanding of men and ideas was too extensive and profound to permit him to identify himself with any narrow or sectarian enthusiasms.

He was already inclined to be a spectator of the pageant of life, a looker-on rather than an actor, but a looker-on whose musings were enriched by much learning and philosophy; for he was indeed a very accomplished young man, extraordinarily well read, of an independent and speculative turn of mind, and, in thought and outlook, fully abreast of the times. He was also, it seems, extremely, but not unpleasantly, self-possessed. One may almost picture him as a sort of Adrian Harley looking on humanity as " a supreme ironic procession, with laughter of gods in the background." But Anatole France possessed what Meredith's " wise youth " conspicuously lacked : that is to say, a heart. And so his wisdom and his irony played like summer lightning, leaving no scar.

Anatole France then was learned, witty, humorous, kindly disposed, a delightful talker, popular with nearly everyone. But learning, culture, a sensitive appreciation of the noble and beautiful things in literature and in life, however valuable they may be for the adornment of the mind, do not, alas ! provide the means of keeping body and soul together. Work had to be done. It would perhaps be scarcely fair to say that Lemerre did not err on the side of generosity towards those who laboured in his vineyard. He was, one understands, a worthy and kindly soul enough ; but he had to make his business pay, and he could not be expected to provide sinecures for poets and philosophers, however attractive their personality. Supplementary occupation of a more or less remunerative character had to be found. It must be remembered that, in those days, reviews and periodical publications were not only few in number, but under strict Government control. To say so much as a word against the Empire meant the prompt suppression of the offending organ. Those who contributed to the principal existing reviews were a body as close and jealous as they were docile and subservient. Docility was not one of Anatole France's outstanding qualities, and editors therefore could not but look on him with suspicion. But it happened that at this time Larousse was bringing out his mighty Dictionary. His office in the Rue Saint André-des-Arts was as busy as an ant-heap, and he had many industrious young literary men working in his service. Among them was Anatole France. Every week he and his friends who had regular jobs on Larousse's staff would present themselves at the office of the " great lexicographer " to deliver into his hands the harvest of their labours and to receive from him their pecuniary reward. Apparently the reward was not always forthcoming Larousse, we are told by Monsieur Xavier de Ricard, was a good-hearted man, " un brave homme," but he had his bad days, his periods of grumpiness and ill humour when he was unapproachable. It was therefore with feelings of uncertainty and misgiving that the band of " collaborateurs " would enter the presence chamber. Besides Lemerre and Larousse there were yet other sources of income, odds and ends that brought a little grist to the mill and it is interesting to note that the future member of the Academy did not disdain, in the days of his youth, to contribute to a cookery book.

Lemerre entertained such a high opinion of young France's literary judgment that after a while he made him his reader. It would be interesting to learn how far this gifted young man with his fastidious literary taste answered the expectations of his employer, and how many " best sellers " he rejected because they offended his classic sense of style. The ideal publisher's reader must necessarily be a Jekyll and Hyde personality, always ready to sacrifice his artistic predilections to his commercial instincts, and it seems hardly probable that Anatole France, who was very little of a business man, could have successfully fulfilled this condition.

Lemerre's was not the sole, or even the first, rendezvous of the Parnassians. They met sometimes at the house of Catulle Mendès, sometimes at Leconte de Lisle's, and sometimes at Théodore de Banville's. Of all these it was Catulle Mendès

ANATOLE FRANCE

*From a portrait by Eugène Carrière, engraved by Ernest Florian.
By permission of M. René Helleu*

who made them most at home. There the atmosphere was free and unrestrained. Not so at Leconte de Lisle's, where, according to Monsieur Xavier de Ricard, they were held in awe by the "monocle sévère du maître Olympien et la menace constante de sa terrible ironie." France was an assiduous attendant at the Mendès salon. "Already," says Monsieur Xavier de Ricard, a nephew of Mendès, "he was an engaging conversationalist, 'well up' in everything and able to speak on every topic without pedantry. He enlivened, and often awakened, discussion by the dexterity of his rejoinders and his arguments and by the unexpected and picturesque turn he would give to the expression of his point of view."

But there was another place, and that more strange and picturesque than any, where the Parnassians, and not they alone, but a motley Bohemian host of men and women interested in the arts, were accustomed to forgather; this was the salon of Madame Nina de Callias, which she, with a pretty wit, used to call her "Charenton"—that is to say, her Bedlam. Nina de Callias inhabited a house of rather imposing appearance at the corner of the Rue Chaptal and the Rue Léonie. Nina herself was as unconventional as she was fascinating, and she seems to have been liberal of her favours, especially to the poets. It is hinted that Anatole France had such good reason to be grateful to her

G

that, if he did not write her poems for her—for she had poetical aspirations—he at least guided the hand that composed them. The vandal years, however, took their inevitable revenge on poor Nina. As her charms and her vivacity forsook her she fell at length on evil days. Poor and lonely, she lived neglected or forgotten by most of those to whom she had given herself and her substance with such heedless prodigality; by most, but not by all, for we may be sure that one, and he the greatest, of her lovers always kept a little chamber in his heart for Nina.

While it was upon his prose work that he depended for his daily bread, it was the poetic muse that he had been courting in his heart. As long ago as his earliest school days, when deep down in his desk he had cherished a note-book containing verses of his own composition entitled "Early Blossoms," he had nourished poetic aspirations. Though Anatole France's most memorable work is not written in verse, he was and is a true poet and his work is greater or less great according to the degree in which the poetic quality is manifested in it. Unless we are profoundly mistaken in our estimate of Monsieur France's work, such books as *My Friend's Book*, *Pierre Nozière*, *The Bloom of Life*, and, in a different order, *Thaïs*, will continue to exert an undiminished charm over the minds of men, when, for all their brilliance, all their wit, *Penguin Island*,

The Revolt of the Angels, perhaps even *La Rôtisserie de la Reine Pédauque* are languishing forgotten on their shelves.

It was not until 1873, after the Franco-Prussian war, that Monsieur France's first volume of poetry —*Poèmes Dorés*—saw the light. It excited but little comment; indeed it fell comparatively flat and yet it contains much that is inspired by true poetic vision and marked by exquisite workmanship. One of the most conspicuous characteristics of Monsieur France's work, whether in poetry or prose, is its translucent clarity, its radiance. Light has ever been sacred to him and the lines in the *Antigone*, in which the chorus of Theban elders address the rising sun, after the besieging Argive host had fled, panic-stricken, in the night : " Beam of the sun, fairest light that ever dawned on Thebé of the Seven Gates, thou hast shone forth at last, eye of the golden day . . ." made upon him a lasting impression, and it is significant that that intellectual radiance, that clear, classic grace which, later on, was to distinguish so much of his prose work, is most apparent in that lyric in which he probably attained the high-water mark of his poetic achievement the *Ode to Light*. " Be Thou," he cries :

Be thou my strength, O Light, may my thought be
   Lucid and fair as Thou ;
Thy grace and peace direct its forward flow,
   Still rhythmical with Thee.

Grant me to see, until my days be told,
  Steeped in all joy and calm,
Beauty move queen-like, over scattered palm,
  Crowned with Thy Virgin gold.

Three years later, in 1876, was published *The Bride of Corinth*, a poetic play in which is described the strife of early Christianity with the waning forces of Paganism. In an exquisite introduction he gives the reader an idea of the subject of his poem and of his treatment of it. "In this book," he says, "I touch on high matters, and delicate to handle; on religious matters. I have dreamed again the dream of the ages of faith; I have illuded myself with lively belief. To have treated what is pious with impiety would have been to lack the sense of harmony. I bring a sincere respect to bear on matters sacred."

"I know," he goes on, "that there is no certainty outside science, but I know also that the worth of scientific truth lies in the methods of its discovery, and that these methods are not to be arrived at by the common run of mankind. It is hardly scientific to hold that science may one day replace religion. So long as man sucks milk of woman, so long will he be consecrated in the temple, and initiated in some sort in divine mystery. He will dream. And what matter if the dream be false, so it be beautiful."

CHAPTER VI

THE MIDDLE YEARS

N the life of such a man as Anatole France it is not the external events that are of the greatest consequence. He has had, indeed, few direct dealings with the world on which he is so illuminating a commentator. The appearance of *The Crime of Sylvestre Bonnard* in 1881 brought him definitely before the general public, to whom, until then, he had been scarcely even a name; but it was not until 1886, when he began, in *Le Temps*, his weekly causeries *On Life and Letters* that his popularity was definitely confirmed. In 1885, however, he had published *My Friend's Book*, a collection of autobiographical reminiscences, set down haphazard and without regard to chronological sequence. This book, which called forth enthusiastic praise from Jules Lemaître, if not the most ambitious, is certainly one of the most delightful products of his pen and, if he had written nothing besides, would suffice to preserve his name from oblivion. On this book and its three sequels,

Pierre Nozière, Little Pierre and *The Bloom of Life*, I have drawn largely for the account I have given of his childhood and adolescence. I have done so with the greater confidence in that I have Monsieur France's assurance that the incidents which I have selected are true in substance and in fact. From the dedication to *My Friend's Book* it will be seen that he had already married. He did in fact wed, in the early eighties, the great-niece of Jean Guérin, the miniaturist of Marie Antoinette. For a time, at any rate, this union went smoothly enough, and we hear praises of home life—of the " douceurs de familles tranquilles," of "travail sous la lampe entre les voix claires d'enfants." Some of the most subtly delicate pages in *My Friend's Book* are inspired by his observation of the ways and antics of his baby daughter. Here, for example, is a little passage whose exquisite and poetic charm it would be difficult to match, even from Anatole France himself :

" ' Just look at her ! ' I cry . . . ' how adorable she looks standing at the drawer there.'

" With a gesture at once mutinous and fearful, her mother came and placed a finger on my lips. Then she went back to the ran·acked drawer (the baby had been rummaging among its contents). Meanwhile I resumed my train of thought.

" ' Dearest, if Suzanne is adorable for what she

knows, she is no less so for what she does not know. It is when her knowledge fails her that her poetry is revealed.'

" At this Suzanne's mamma turned her eyes upon me, smiling a little mocking smile out of the corner of her mouth.

" ' Suzanne's poetry,' she cried, ' your daughter's poetry ? Why, she's only happy when she's in the kitchen, that daughter of yours. I found her grubbing among the potato peelings the other day, as happy as a queen. You call that poetry, do you ? '

" ' Most certainly, my dear, most certainly ! All Nature is mirrored in her eyes with so magnificent a purity that, for her, nothing in the world is dirty, not even the refuse-basket. Therefore it is, that you discovered her rapt in wondering admiration of cabbage leaves, onion skins, and shrimps' tails. It was a delicious experience for her. I assure you she transmutes Nature with heavenly alchemy, and whatever she sees or touches is instinct with beauty in her eyes.'

" During this harangue, Suzanne quitted the chest of drawers and went to the window. Her mother followed her and took her in her arms. The lovely tresses of the acacia whose blossom lay in trails of white about our courtyard were bathed in translucent darkness. The dog was sleeping with his front paws outside his kennel. Far and wide the earth lay drenched in liquid azure. We all three held our peace.

"Then, amid the silence, Suzanne raised her arms as high as she could above her, and with her finger, which she could never stretch quite straight, she pointed to a star. This finger—a miracle of tiny loveliness—she would bend at intervals as though she were beckoning to something.

"Then Suzanne talked to the star.

"What she told it was not made up of words; it was a language obscure and lovely, a sort of strange runic chant, something sweet yet profoundly mysterious, as is befitting to express the soul of a baby, when a star is mirrored in it."

A charming picture of domestic bliss, of conjugal felicity. And if it was not fated to endure, if the fear of Nemesis which Madame France, *née* Guérin, perpetually entertained was not groundless, whom or what shall we blame but the Fates who united her with a man whom, at that stage of his career at least, this comfortable home-keeping happiness could but imperfectly satisfy?

The only child of this marriage, Suzanne, was twice married, first to Capitaine Mollins and secondly to Michel Psichari, a grandson of Ernest Renan. Michel Psichari died the death of a hero in the Great War. His widow did not long survive him. The loss of her husband weighed heavily

upon her and she died of influenza in 1918. Their
only child, young Lucien Psichari, lives with
Monsieur and Madame France at La Béchellerie.
The boy is a sort of Absalom in the eyes of his
grandfather, and it appears that there is nothing
he may not have for the asking. The Master
told me rather an amusing story in which young
Lucien played an important part. At the time
of the canonization of Joan of Arc there were
great festivities at Tours, and all the houses in and
about the city were beflagged and illuminated.
Lucien asked if he might undertake the illumination
of the house and grounds of La Béchellerie. The
Master gave his consent, and the result was, all
the other houses in the neighbourhood which were
illumined in honour of St. Joan, were easily out-
shone by the lights of La Béchellerie, the home
of Anatole France, the sceptical philosopher. There
was something deliciously paradoxical about the
story that brought the merriest twinkle into the old
man's eyes as he related it.

Apart from the publication of his successive works,
which are dealt with later on in this study, the next
external event of importance in the career of Anatole
France took place in 1896. On the 24th December
of that year he was elected a member of the Académie
française, filling the chair made vacant by the death
of Ferdinand de Lesseps. Since *My Friend's Book*,

which appeared in 1885, Monsieur France had published, among other minor works, *Balthasar*, a volume of short stories, in 1889, *Thaïs* in 1890, the four series of *Life and Letters* in 1891-2, *Mother of Pearl* in 1892, *At the Sign of the Reine Pédauque* and *The Opinions of M. Jérôme Coignard* in 1893, *The Red Lily* in 1894, *The Garden of Epicurus* and *The Well of St. Clare* in 1895. These books form a body of achievement of such undeniable merit, their author's literary fame was so securely established not only in France but in Europe, that his exclusion from that august institution which is looked upon in France as the arbiter of taste and the guardian of tradition in the sphere of letters, would, so at least it appears to us to-day, have been almost unthinkable. Ferdinand Fabre, the rival candidate, was opposed by the clericals. The future champion of Monsieur Combes, the future author of *Penguin Island* and *Vers les Temps Meilleurs*, had not yet declared himself very definitely on his attitude towards the Church. The general impression gained from what he had hitherto written, such, for example, as his essay on " Mysticism and Science," in the fourth volume of his *Life and Letters*, and his sympathetic, almost tender handling of sacred matters in *The Crime of Sylvestre Bonnard*, *My Friend's Book*, and *Mother of Pearl*, probably gave rise to the view that, whatever convictions he might hold in his heart, he was never likely to show himself as lacking, at all events externally, in those qualities of *pietas* and *urbanitas*, those essentially Latin qualities, that were well calculated to make him *persona grata* with the Academy.

It was no doubt pretty generally held that if, as Monsieur de Bonnières has said, Anatole France, like Renan, had dropped most of his beliefs, he had at all events retained a taste, an affection for many of them.

From the opinion which Monsieur Jérôme Coignard confided to his alumnus, Jacques Tourne-broche, we may form a fairly accurate idea of Anatole France's attitude towards the august and erudite company to whom his name was to impart an added lustre. It would appear, however, if all reports be true, that his behaviour in the sessions of the Immortals was not invariably distinguished by the sedateness and decorum befitting in one who should be privileged to participate in the deliberations of such an Olympian society. There is extant a malicious story, which may indeed be mythical, though it is to be hoped it is not, a story which would make out Monsieur France to be a true spiritual descendant of François Rabelais, to whom it owes its inspiration. The Immortals were engaged upon the revision of the Dictionary and had reached the word " anneau." Great care had been bestowed

upon the definition of this word—as upon all the
words that had preceded it—in order that no use
of it, however remote or unusual, should be over-
looked. The various meanings were at length
considered to have been duly recorded, when
Anatole France nudged his neighbour, whose naive
innocence was as great as his learning, which, though
it did not appear to include an acquaintance with
Rabelais, was prodigious. " Tell them," whispered
Anatole France, " they've forgotten the ring of
Hans Carvel." " Eh ! what ring ? " asked the
old gentleman, who was rather deaf. " Why, the
ring of Hans Carvel ! " repeated Anatole France,
who declined his colleague's invitation to draw
attention to the omission himself on the ground
of the shyness natural in a new member. Thereupon
the aged and highly respected savant rose up and
said, to the consternation of all the members, who
thought that his brain must have given way beneath
the weight of his erudition, and that he had suddenly
become the victim of a distressing and obscene form
of mental aberration : " But, messieurs, have you
then forgotten the ring of Hans Carvel ? "

But there was now about to occur an event which
was to have on Anatole France, on his work and on
his attitude to life, an influence of which it is
difficult to estimate the full importance. That
event was the stupendous conspiracy against the

laws of justice and common humanity which is known as the Dreyfus case. It is unnecessary to recapitulate here the various stages of that incredible and sombre tragedy. The name of Titus Oates is not branded with deeper or more lasting infamy than are those of Esterhazy and Henry, forgers and perjurers, who were the arch-villains in this base and hideous attempt to compass the ruin of an innocent man. Anatole France, as is evident from his writings, was not and never had been, visited by any particular tenderness towards the Jews, but he was, for all his dilettantism, a staunch upholder of Justice, a resolute champion of the oppressed. It was on the 13th of January, 1898, that Zola published his famous letter " J'accuse." Shortly afterwards a petition for a re-trial was launched under the title " Protestation des Intellectuels," and Anatole France was among the first to sign it. This document was the signal for a tremendous outburst of popular hatred. One has to go back to the descriptions of the Gordon riots to gain an idea of the violence, the ungovernable rage of the mob. The country was convulsed by the upheaval, at which the whole civilized world looked on in amazement. The pitiable, the egregious obstinacy of the authorities is shown by the fact that, though the Court of Cassation annulled the decision of the court-martial in 1899, though a second military trial resulted in the grotesque verdict of " Guilty with extenuating circumstances," and though President Loubet was pleased to pardon the prisoner for a crime which it was now obvious to all he had never committed, another six years were to elapse before the terrible ceremony of Dreyfus's degradation was reversed and the martyr of Devil's Island was formally reinstated in the Army. The attitude of Anatole France to the Dreyfus affair is reflected in the four volumes of *L'Histoire Contemporaine*, which appeared during its progress ; and in *Penguin Island* that irony, which had hitherto been so gay and debonair, grows sombre and bitter under the influence of this overwhelming national disaster which had exposed his country to the contemptuous pity of the world. The depths of human meanness and bigotry had been sounded, and it had been his own countrymen that had sounded them. Anatole France had quitted his Tower of Ivory. It has not been given to him to return to it, at least permanently. He took part actively, as a politician, not remotely as a spectator or a philosopher, in championing the cause of the proletariat. That poise, that balance, that taste which used to be so delicate, so unerring, is henceforth liable to occasional disturbance. He expresses himself sometimes with a violence which, whatever indication it may afford of his sincerity and his zeal, comes

strangely from the creator of that most genial and
imperturbable of philosophers, the Abbé Jérôme
Coignard. Henceforth, forgetting his old canon
about treating pious things in a spirit of piety, he
poses—and perhaps the word is not altogether
ill-chosen—as the implacable enemy of the *parti
noir*, of the black-coated brigade, as we might
call the clergy. Henceforth we shall find him,
so long as his health will permit, at every public
demonstration of his friends the socialists. Public
notices and posters of whose style he can scarcely
approve will be found to bear his signature. He
will take the chair at dinners and gatherings and
election meetings, at working-men's socials; he
will open co-operative restaurants, communist print-
ing presses and all manner of similar enterprises.
"Ah, well," he recently said to me, "in politics
one must take a definite side, in politics there is
no room for philosophic doubt." It may be so.
Yet it is none the less strange to find this lover of
the past, this child of the Muses, this gentle philosopher, ranging himself thus with the iconoclasts,
with the scorners of tradition. What has become
of the Anatole France who bade us "not lightly cast
aside anything that belongs to the Past, because
only with the Past can we rear the fabric of the
Future"? Nay, what has become of that genial
pessimist who was indifferent to all changes of

government and all reforms because he noticed " that the course of life is in no way changed, and after reforms men are, as before, selfish, avaricious, cowardly, cruel, stupid and furious by turns, and there is always a nearly even number of births, marriages, cuckolds and gallows-birds, in which is made manifest the beautiful ordering of our society ".?

CHAPTER VII

TRAVELS IN FRANCE AND ABROAD

NATOLE FRANCE has been a great traveller. Italy and Spain he knows almost as well as his own country, and of the latter there is no corner with which he is unfamiliar. If you would know in what the true patriotic spirit consists, if you would acquaint yourself with the patriotism of a poet deeply versed in the annals of his country, you would do well to read the "Promenades de Pierre Nozière en France," which form the third part of the volume entitled *Pierre Nozière*. "What are towns," he exclaims, "but books in very truth—books adorned with gracious pictures wherein we may discern the faces of our forefathers?" He thrills at the sight of a storied building, an historic town or city, as a lover thrills at the sight of his mistress's face. "Here, in Valois," he says, "sweetness and calm are upon the land. Gladly would I kiss the very soil. . . .

H   97

Generation after generation has come and gone and left its abiding mark upon it, so that, virginal and radiant as it is with the loveliness of youth, it is yet the ancient reliquary of our race." The ear of Anatole France is sensitively attuned to the voices of the Past, he can catch the message whispered by the gracious and venerable things of antiquity, the

> ". . . musical but melancholy chime
> Which they can hear who meddle not with crime,
> Nor avarice, nor over-anxious care."

His travels in the Mediterranean countries were undertaken for his own pleasure. But in 1909, from April to September, he went on a lecturing tour to the Argentine. Alas, Anatole France is no orator, and the best that can be said of these lectures is that they were but a qualified success. The subject he chose for his discourses, Rabelais, seemed to have no particular interest for his public. Moreover, the Archbishop of Buenos Ayres denounced him in a sort of pontificial edict. No women attended his lectures, and an audience without women is bound to be somewhat lugubrious. He also lectured in Brazil, but there too he met with no better success; and it may be said of him, as of Matthew Arnold, that he did not shine as a popular lecturer.

In December, 1913, the Master paid a brief but

memorable visit to this country. The central event of his sojourn in London was the banquet given in his honour at the Savoy Hotel. On this occasion it was apparently decided, in those remote and exalted circles where such decisions are made, that the socialist should be ignored (his turn was to come later, with the Fabians), but that honour could and should be paid to the man of genius, the foremost man of letters of the day. The feast was therefore presided over by a peer, the late Lord Redesdale, himself a gifted writer. The company was numerous and distinguished. High politics and high finance were abundantly, if somewhat incongruously, represented. The scene was also graced by many of the brightest luminaires in the literary firmament. Thomas Hardy was unfortunately prevented from attending. The following letter from him, addressed to Mr. John Lane, was read by the chairman :

" I particularly regret that, though one of the Committee, I am unable to be present to meet Monsieur Anatole France at the reception on Wednesday. In these days, when the literature of narrative and verse seems to be losing its qualities as an art, and to be assuming a structureless, conglomerate character, it is a privilege that we should have come into our midst a writer who is faithful to the principles that make for permanence, who

never forgets the value of organic form and sym-
metry, the force of reserve, and the emphasis of
under-statement, even in his lighter works."

Luckily, however, both Miss Marie Corelli and
Mr. Jerome K. Jerome, in whose works, even the
lightest, "the emphasis of under-statement" is not
conspicuous, were able to display their catholicity
of spirit by paying their tribute to a writer with
whom they have so little in common. Except for
the circumstance that I had paid for my ticket, my
title to be included among the company was frail
and insignificant. Politics, finance knew me not;
but I knew half a dozen or so of Monsieur France's
works almost by heart, and I had translated two
of them into English. And so I crept, a
shrinking stowaway, into this gilded and magnificent galley. Monsieur France, though an inimit-
able talker, is not a speaker, and on this occasion
he read his discourse. All that I now remember
of it was the rich, deliberate music of the voice
that uttered it, and the words which he repeated
with strange insistency: "*Travaillons de concert
à la paix du monde*"—"Let us work together
for the peace of the world." This was in December,
1913. The exhortation, thus reiterated, seemed
even then to be fraught with ominous significance,
and now, looking back over the years of horror
that were so soon to follow, one wonders whether

this old man with his strange, inscrutable eyes and musical, melancholy voice had somehow seen the shadow of the coming catastrophe.

At once affable and distant, courteous and remote, was the bearing of the Master as, one by one, the long file of celebrities bore down upon him. Politics and finance and the " best sellers " of the day having paid their devoirs to genius, the greater planets and the fixed stars having duly coruscated, I now advanced, a timid and anonymous atom of the Milky Way. Carried away by a sudden gust of audacity, as sometimes happens to the very shy, I ventured on a little flight of fancy. " *Cher maître*," said I, " I have known you ever since you were so high." And I put my hand down to the level of my knee. As Monsieur France turned a rather puzzled glance upon me, as one who should say to himself, " Is the fellow mad ? " I hurriedly added that I had translated into English those two books of his, *My Friend's Book* and *Pierre Nozière*, in which he tells the story of his childish days : how he used to wander along the Quai Malaquais hand in hand with his old nurse, Nanette ; how he pored over his old picture Bible beneath the lamp's soft light at his father's table ; how he went to the Jardin des Plantes and thought it was the Garden of Eden, and so forth.

Observing my drift, he took my hand in both of

his and smiled a smile of such kindly warmth that the glow of it is with me yet.

The reception by the Fabian Society took place at the Suffolk Galleries. Mr. Bernard Shaw was in the chair. When Anatole France rose to make his speech, he began with the customary " Mesdames et Messieurs," and then, turning to Bernard Shaw, he added with a bow and a smile, " et le Molière d'Angleterre ! " When France had finished there came eulogistic orations from Shaw, Keir Hardie and H. M. Hyndman. Anatole France then rose to reply.

When he had finished his discourse there was enacted a strange, indeed a unique, incident. Anatole France is not, in the ordinary sense, accounted a man of action, but on this historic occasion he performed a deed so startling, so dazzling, that in one brief moment he may be said to have redeemed the physical inertia of a lifetime. Advancing with outstretched hands towards " the Molière of England," he flung his arms about his neck and imprinted a kiss upon each of his blushing cheeks. If a thunderbolt had crashed upon the stage it could not have created greater wonderment among the serried ranks of Fabians than did the scarcely audible impact of this unprecedented osculation. Mr. Shaw—the insouciant, the imperturbable Mr. Shaw—visibly wilted, but only for a second.

Recovering himself instantly, he dauntlessly and gracefully returned the salute, amid the tempestuous plaudits of the throng.

"Mark Rutherford" somewhere refers to the most remarkable embraces in history: Joseph falling on Israel's neck; Paul embraced by the elders at Ephesus; Romeo embracing Juliet in the vault and sealing the doors of breath with a righteous kiss; Penelope embracing Ulysses after his wanderings; but he considers none of these more remarkable than that on the *Abercorn Arms* at Stanmore when King George IV of England exchanged kisses with Louis XVIII of France. Had he enjoyed the good fortune to behold it, he might have considered the embrace of Anatole France and Bernard Shaw as more remarkable still.

After this, even so important an event as Monsieur France's visit to No. 10 Downing Street, may come as something of an anti-climax. Mr. Asquith, who was then Prime Minister, was unfortunately not at home—the visit was an unpremeditated one. In his absence the honours were performed by Mrs. Asquith. It cannot, however, be doubted that the wisest and wittiest of living French writers must have deeply valued the opportunity of conversing with this brilliant Englishwoman whose wit is only equalled by her indiscretion.

CHAPTER VIII

THE NOBEL PRIZE AND THE INDEX

N 1921 Anatole France was awarded the Nobel Prize in recognition of his invaluable contributions to literature. It was the outward and visible act which ratified and confirmed that pre-eminence in the world of letters which all people of taste, whose judgment was not warped by nationalist prejudices and narrow jealousies, had long since tacitly accorded him.

As for the value Monsieur France himself set upon the prize, he said :

"Unless one is occupied with literature merely as literature—and who is so occupied?—those things which most confer authority are valuable. I am grateful to a jury whose reputation for impartiality is held in such high esteem.

"Its decisions possess an international value, and I rejoice in it, for it is a confirmation of what is, for me, the principal lesson of the war : the beneficent influence exerted by intellectual intercourse with other countries."

Anatole France, who went to Stockholm to receive the prize, retains the happiest impressions of his visit. " Sweden," he says, " is a charming country, and no city ever pleases me more than Stockholm." He found much to interest him and to delight the eye in the royal palace and the museums, but above all he was exhilarated by the " air pacifique et frais " of the northern capital. The royal family were lavish in their attentions to the illustrious and venerable socialist. It was pointed out to him that the King, so beloved of his people, displayed neither the pomp nor the *hauteur* of a Republican President. " I did not forget," commented the Master, " that the King of Sweden was a Bernadotte. But he is accustomed to power. A President, on the other hand, always strikes one as a little new at the game. He hasn't had time to get *blasé*."

On his way home he stayed for a brief while in Berlin, where he was visited by the famous Einstein. " I am not enough of a mathematician," said Monsieur France, " to understand his system, and I was modest enough not to talk to him about it. The great Einstein," he added characteristically, " is lost in the gravitation of the stars, and so our little terrestrial agitations leave him undisturbed."

In the early autumn of 1922, the literary and intellectual world was startled by the news that the

works of Anatole France—all of them : *The Crime
of Sylvestre Bonnard* as well as *Penguin Island ;
Mother of Pearl* as well as *Vers les Temps Meilleurs*—
had without exception or discrimination been
formally placed on the Index. In this country
there is naturally some tendency to regard decisions
of the Roman Curia with indifference, if not with
levity. Nobody, people are inclined to think, is
" one penny the worse." On the contrary, it is a
valuable advertisement for an author, and is bound
to attract popular attention to his work. This is perhaps a short-sighted and rather insular view, and it is
probable that in countries where the Puritan ideal
burns less brightly than in our own, the formal
condemnation of the Church is regarded with less
equanimity. Nevertheless, it must be confessed
that in delivering so sweeping a judgment, the
ecclesiastical authorities do seem to have gone
unnecessarily far. If they had restricted the mani-
festation of their disapproval to the more violent
of Monsieur France's communist and anti-clerical
utterances, in which, if the voice is the voice of the
Master, the sentiments and language are sometimes
those of the market-place orator, they would have
done a real service to literature, inasmuch as they
would have done something to winnow the spurious
France from the true.

It is regrettable that this penalty should have been

called for in respect of that part of his work that will certainly prove ephemeral. Even now, the bulk of the French reading public do not always take the political fulminations of Monsieur France very seriously. "The fact is," (this is the sort of thing they say), "he has allowed a lot of dubious people to get hold of him, people who exploit him for their own ends. Well, if he wants to amuse himself in this way, let him. It's just his hobby. We know the real France. *Him* we all love and admire. *He* is the Anatole France that will live." To this view we do not entirely subscribe. We believe that in all his political utterances Anatole France is perfectly sincere ; and that he is moved principally by pity for the masses whose lot he makes it his endeavour to ameliorate. This it is that gives the key to the enigma of his character. Nor does he hesitate, when occasion demands it, to give resolute expression to opinions which he knows are calculated to incur the disapproval, if not the detestation, of the vast majority of his compatriots. Of this his attitude over the Dreyfus case was a convincing example ; and, later, when he went to receive the Nobel Prize at Stockholm, he is reported to have delivered himself of the following dictum concerning the Treaty of Versailles, which, to say the least, must have sounded unpleasantly in the ears of those multitudes who—at the moment—still regard Mon-

sieur Poincaré as the invincible champion of their
country's just rights : " The most horrible of wars,"
said Monsieur France, " was followed by a treaty
which was not a treaty of peace, but a prolongation
of the war.   The downfall of Europe is inevitable
unless at long last the spirit of reason is imported
into its councils."   This declaration evoked a storm
of   protest.   That   perfervid   patriot,   Monsieur
Gustave Hervé, could no longer contain himself,
and he laid about him with a will.

" There is nothing to be surprised at in this
statement," he said, " for those who know their
Anatole France.   That delightful sceptic, with his
morbid   artistic   sensibility,   his   rebellious   spirit
which would have made him so powerful a dissolvent
if he had possessed Voltaire's passionate soul, has
long chosen to range himself with the partisans of
the extreme Left in opposition to the men and ideas
of the extreme Right.   That is the man's Church,
and Cachin is his spiritual director.   He would
sooner have had Jaurés, but Jaurés is dead.   He
follows the herd, dragged along by his little band of
admirers. : . . The unfortunate thing is that, for
a host of worthy folk, men like Anatole France,
Gorki and Wells, who, outside their own particular
art, are nothing but poor creatures like the rest,
nevertheless carry weight even when they open their
mouths to speak of matters of which they obviously
know absolutely nothing.

MONSIEUR AND MADAME FRANCE

*From a photograph taken by M. Henry Davray at the entrance to the Library
at La Béchellerie*

" And now you have the French people choosing this celebrity, with his timorousness and his hesitations, to pronounce on such questions as those that are crying for solution at Versailles. It is so easy to criticize, and he is so marvellous when he plays the critic. But when there's something to be done, some decision to be made, I would rather have Clemenceau."

That is the present view of Pecus as voiced by Monsieur Gustave Hervé. Well,

" Let Hercules himself do what he may,
The cat will mew and the dog will have his day . . ."

Time will perhaps show that, as Monsieur Bergeret has said, the power of thought is greater than the sword, and that truth, which is not always with those who shout the loudest, will, in the long run, prevail—even against the big battalions.

All that now remains to be added to this record of the outstanding events in the life of the Master is that he was married in September 1920 to Mademoiselle Emma Laprevotte, a gentle and kindly lady who surrounds her illustrious husband with every care, and who is endowed in a supreme degree with the gift of making her visitors seem thoroughly at home.

As has often been remarked, no great writer has ever put more of his personality into his books than has Anatole France. In them he has built for himself a monument more durable than brass.

The second part of this essay will be devoted to a survey of his work as a poet, critic, novelist, short-story writer and historian, together with some considerations regarding his philosophy and his literary style.

PART II

ANATOLE FRANCE
HIS WORK

CHAPTER IX

THE NOVELIST

I

MONSIEUR FRANCE'S first essay in fiction dates back to 1879, when he published, in a single volume, two stories entitled *Jocasta* and *The Famished Cat.* They need not delay us long. Here and there they give hints of the talent that later was to manifest itself triumphantly; but for the most part they are too derivative to merit detailed attention. It is to be noted that the first edition of this volume was preceded by a preface which was subsequently suppressed. That preface contained a little story entitled " André," which was afterwards included, with some interesting modifications, in *My Friend's Book.*

It was not until 1881, when he was thirty-seven, that Monsieur France attained the ear of the *grand public. The Crime of Sylvestre Bonnard,* which saw the light in that year, at once achieved a considerable, though not an overwhelming, popular success. It

was crowned by the Academy. Of all Monsieur
France's books it is probably now the most widely
read, which is not surprising, since it is not his best.
But it appeals to all ages and all conditions and—
of set purpose—offends the susceptibilities of none.
Only such as have heard that Monsieur France deals
rather frankly with questions of sex are likely to
experience disappointment. It contains none of
those fleshly incidents which the Victorians roundly
called " improper " and we, of the present generation, merely " daring." This might have been
thought to impose a serious handicap on its chances
of success. But there is one quality which is even
more securely entrenched in popular favour than
impropriety, and that is sentimentality. And *The
Crime of Sylvestre Bonnard* is unquestionably
sentimental.

My Friend's Book and its sequels, *Pierre Nozière,
Little Pierre,* and *The Bloom of Life,* deal with
Monsieur France's childhood and adolesence from
the point of view of mature or advanced age ; *The
Crime of Sylvestre Bonnard* is an imaginary portrait of
the author as an old man, drawn by himself in early
manhood ; a picture of himself as he was fain to be
when his labours in the field of scholarship and the
passage of the years should have brought him a sufficient competence, wisdom, the respect of his colleagues, academic honours and a European reputation

for learning. But Pierre Nozière has this advan-
tage over Sylvestre Bonnard : he is an authentic
person, illumined indeed by the imagination, softened
and idealized by the magic touch of memory, but,
in essence, unmistakably real and true; whereas
Monsieur Bonnard, being an artificial projection
of the author's self into a wholly imaginary future, resembles one of those terrifying forms which travellers
sometimes see outlined upon the clouds in lands of
mists and mountains, and which are in reality but
the magnified and distorted image of themselves.
For Sylvestre Bonnard is a monster, a monster not
indeed of vice, but of virtue. This dear old scholar,
who remains true to the memory of Clémentine,
his first and only love—though she has disdained
him for an over-ambitious bank-clerk—who lived
alone with an old housekeeper, of course as
tyrannical as she was loyal; this kindly old fellow
who, by a strange turn of fate, falls in with the
daughter (in the later editions she is the grand-
daughter) of Clémentine, abducts her from a board-
ing establishment where, with the cognisance of a
scoundrelly notary, her legal guardian, she is being
maltreated and exploited by a bitter and designing
schoolmistress; and who finally decides to sell his
beloved books to provide the child with a dowry—
this dear old gentleman is so kindly, so gentle, so
unselfish and so unreal that we are led to wonder

whether or not we are contemplating some product of the fertile but sentimental imagination of Sir J. M. Barrie, one of those beneficent beings endowed with supernatural *naïveté* and wisdom who come to set things right for the naughty wayward little people who inhabit this imperfect world. To speak quite plainly, Sylvestre Bonnard would be a great deal better if he were not quite so good. Though we may deplore that Clémentine elected to marry Noël Alexandre, the bank-clerk, rather than the blameless young student, Sylvestre Bonnard, we confess we can understand it.

The work is called a " roman," but, even in the widest acceptation of the term, it can scarcely be so defined. It is rather a study of the character of Sylvestre Bonnard illumined, brought out into relief, by two episodes having no connection one with the other. Thus the construction is faulty, or rather construction there is none. Construction is not Monsieur France's strong point. His genius is episodic and his characters are, so to speak, ready-made ; they are not developed or expanded by the action of events. Events, incidents, situations are employed to illumine them after the manner of the limelight in a theatre. Sylvestre Bonnard is as upright and benevolent, Mademoiselle Préfère as despicable and designing, Maître Mouche as scoundrelly and hypocritical—no more so and no less —at the beginning as at the end of the narrative.

Nunc dimittis servum tuum, Domine, says the old man at the end of the story. His life's work is done. He has lived long enough to bring happiness into the life of Jeanne the orphan child—or grandchild—of his beloved Clémentine, whose memory he has never ceased to cherish; he has sold his books, or most of them—some he retained against the dictates of his conscience, and this, not, as many think, the abduction, was his crime—to provide Jeanne with a dowry; he has lived to see her happily married, and to stand godfather to her children. His eyes have beheld all the happiness which he can hope for, and so he prays, "Lord, now lettest thou thy servant depart in peace." It is a touching and beautiful conclusion wrought in the romantico-sentimental style which—perhaps rather regrettably—went out with the last century. One is reminded of the *Adsum* of Colonel Newcome. Well, the servant was dismissed. But we need have no misgivings. He will come back again, *sed quantum mutatus ab illo!* How changed, indeed, from his contact with the world. Nicias, the sceptical Epicurean, the dissolute old Abbé Jérôme Coignard, Doctor Trublet—strange metamorphoses, these, of the virtuous Monsieur Bonnard. Perhaps Monsieur Bergeret, professor at the Sorbonne, resembles him most closely; but many things, and notably the charms of Madame de Gromance, preserved Monsieur Bergeret from the præterhuman perfection that we find so disquieting in Monsieur Bonnard.

Of course the swarm of " peepers and botanizers " who follow in the wake of every great writer, and who combine the industry of the ant with the voracity of the locust, lost no time in getting to work. Once more they have made the discovery that there is no new thing under the sun. In Sylvestre Bonnard Monsieur France, it seems, has drawn for style or matter on Renan, Beaudelaire, Mérimée, Theuriet. Indeed, Theuriet in *l'Abbé Daniel* supplies the central idea for the *Crime of Sylvestre Bonnard*. Theuriet's hero became a priest because his cousin had disdained his love. Later on he befriends her daughter, whom she had left an orphan, marries her to one of his pupils, is happy in their happiness and, like Sylvestre Bonnard, when his work is done, says with a wistful sigh, *Nunc dimittis servum tuum, Domine*. That a disappointed lover should become a priest, or a soldier, or even an explorer, is in accordance with the romantic tradition. That he should settle down as a contented old scholar absorbed in antiquarian research is perhaps less so. It may be that Sylvestre Bonnard, like Anatole France, was an Epicurean even in his disappointments. " I noticed," says Monsieur France in *The Bloom of Life*, " that my comrades' passions were violent, whilst mine were gentle; that they

suffered from theirs, whilst I enjoyed mine." It
is a happy frame of mind, and though it consorts
ill with *la grande passion*, it is admirably adapted
to that elegant eighteenth-century sentimentality
traditionally associated with bundles of faded love
letters, harpsichords, high-waists and pot-pourri.

But when every reservation is made, how full
the book remains of delicate thought and exquisite
expression ! The very form of it, which is that
of a personal diary, is calculated to conceal, almost
to make a virtue of, its weakness of construction.
The praise accorded to it by the Academy in their
official report is not exaggerated. " The *naïveté*
of the scholar, his ingenuousness of soul, his kindness
of heart, are charmingly portrayed. The narrative
is full of life and the interest well-sustained. If
the style is not always free from preciosity, the
workmanship is, for the most part, sound, elegant
and correct. It has been the desire of the Academy
to honour by an exceptional award a delicate and
distinguished work which is itself, perhaps, as exceptional as the award bestowed upon it." " Perhaps
as exceptional." The words seem to convey the idea
that some one had at least a presentiment that the
author of *The Crime of Sylvestre Bonnard* might
prove to be a very great artist indeed. The confirmation of that impression was destined to be
delayed for nearly nine years, for it was assuredly

not reinforced by *The Aspirations of Jean Servien*, which appeared the following year. Though the exact date of its composition seems a little doubtful, it was certainly written long before *The Crime of Sylvestre Bonnard*.

But in 1890 there appeared, from the pen of Monsieur Anatole France, a work which, if he had written no other, would have sufficed to have placed its author in the forefront of his own, or indeed of any generation. *The Crime of Sylvestre Bonnard* he wrote—one cannot help thinking—to please the public. It was a conscious and a successful bid for popularity. *Thaïs* he wrote to please himself, to please the poet, the artist, the philosopher, the cultured voluptuary that was within him. It moves with all the triumphant sweep of a great and genuine inspiration. It is an epic of the eternal struggle between the spirit and the senses. The mere story—which is adapted from an old tradition —would have been of little importance had not the writer by the power of genius given it a universal and eternal application. A laborious and conscientious archæologist may delve into the records of the past and produce a cold inventory, an exact but lifeless reconstruction of the incidents of a bygone age, and of the scenes amid which they were enacted. No one who had not had experience within himself of the conflict of soul and sense of which *Thaïs* is

the expression could have written as Anatole France
has written, or have endowed his characters with
the living reality with which they come before us.
He has awakened these sleepers from their centuries
of slumber, he has recreated the scenes amid which
they lived, not with the inhuman aloofness of the
archæologist or the antiquary, but with the insight
of the poet who can read the secrets of the heart.
Anatole France knows life, and the breath of life
informs these pages. Sensuous, musical with the
sound of lyres and flutes, sweet with the perfume
of roses, lit with the glow of imperishable dawns,
such is the setting of the stage on which the anchorite
of the desert and the courtesan of Alexandria enact
their tragic parts.

Moralists are an eager, unquiet race, and they
will always be asking of this book or of that, " What
does it teach ? " "What had the author in mind
when he wrote it ? " He probably wrote *Thaïs*
because he had to beat out the music and to paint
the visions that were within him. But if this is too
vague, if a definite purpose must be assigned to
the work, it seems to me that that purpose is to
inculcate the μηδὲν ἄγαν of Theognis. It is, in
effect, if not by design, a protest against that fanaticism, that lack of balance, of moderation, which is
the arch-enemy of all beauty. In Paphnutius we
are shown all the deformity which fanaticism

produces in the mind and soul. But those who would say that Anatole France presents Paphnutius as the normal type of Christian are grievously in error. No one more than the author of *Mother of Pearl* could be more sensitive to the grace and loveliness of the Christian faith. And where is the beauty of Christian humility more touchingly portrayed than in the picture contained in this very book of the hermit Palaemon, whose hands the wild creatures of the desert came and licked. But with fanaticism, which is gloomy and bitter, which would banish joy and beauty from the world, and which is really the offspring of selfishness and pride, with this attitude of mind, whether in its ancient or modern manifestations, whether it is exhibited by an anchorite of the third century or a narrow ultramontanist of to-day, Anatole France is perpetually at variance. Yet even so, his philosophy, his breadth of vision, his serenity save him from meeting violence with violence. Says Nicias, addressing Paphnutius, of whom he had once been the friend—Nicias, the sceptical, epicurean philosopher, in whom every reader will recognise Anatole France himself—" My dear Paphnutius, do not imagine that I think you extremely absurd, or even altogether unreasonable. And if I were to compare your life with mine, I could not say which is preferable in itself. I shall presently go and take the

bath which Crobyle and Myrtale have prepared
for me; I shall eat the wing of a Phasian pheasant;
then I shall read—for the hundredth time—some
fable by Apuleius, or some treatise by Porphyry.
You will return to your cell, where, leaning like
a tame camel, you will ruminate on I know not
what formulas of incantations you have long chewed
and rechewed, and in the evening you will swallow
some radishes without any oil. Well, dear friend,
in accomplishing these acts so different in appearance, we are both obeying the same sentiment,
the same and the only motive of all human actions;
we are both seeking our own pleasure and striving
to attain the same end—happiness, impossible
happiness. It would be folly on my part to say
you were wrong, dear friend, even though I think
myself in the right.

"And you, my Thaïs, go and enjoy yourself,
and be more happy still, if it be possible, in abstinence
and austerity, than you have been in riches and
pleasure. On the whole I should say you were to
be envied. For if, in our whole lives, Paphnutius and
I have pursued but one kind of pleasurable satisfaction, you in your life, dear Thaïs, have tasted
joys of such opposite characters as it is seldom given
to the same person to know. I should really like
to be for one hour a saint, like our dear friend
Paphnutius. But that is not possible. Farewell,

then, Thaïs ! Go where the secret forces of nature
and your destiny conduct you ! Go, and whither-
soever you go, take with you the good wishes of
Nicias ! I know how empty is the gift, but can I
give you aught save vain regrets and fruitless wishes
in payment for the delicious illusions which formerly
enveloped me within your arms, and whereof the
shadow still is mine ? ''

There, indeed, is the mild voice of tolerance.
smiling, kindly tolerance, with just a hint of irony,
But how salutary a doctrine for those saints whose
sanctity is at least one half pride ; how usefully
to be pondered :

> " When the soul, mounting higher,
> To God comes no nigher ;
> But the arch-fiend Pride
> Mounts at her side . . .''

The ascetic, the iconoclast, those who would destroy
the loveliness of the pagan world and demolish its
temples, strip its altars, sweep away its beliefs, with
these Monsieur France is not in sympathy ; but even
of these he can speak charitably, as of that Saint
Valery who made war so fiercely upon the nymphs of
the woods and streams ; and made war in vain ; for,
says Monsieur France through the mouth of Pierre
Nozière, " As long as there are woods and meadows,
as long as the mountains and the lakes and the rivers
endure, and the white morning mists upgather

and wreathe themselves above the running brooks,
so long will the nymphs and the dryads and the
fairies live on. They are the beauty of the world
and will never perish." But then Valery, despite
his onslaught on the little pagan gods, was a different
order of saint from Paphnutius. To begin with,
he was a worker, a pioneer who taught his brethren
to till the soil, to clear the forest and to drain the
marsh—*laborare est orare* was his watchword! Moreover, it is said of him, as later on it was said of St.
Francis of Assisi, that he bestowed even upon dumb
creatures the loving pity of which his heart was full.
The little birds used to come and eat from his
hand.

It will be seen that a considerable difference
marked the Anatole France of *The Crime of Sylvestre
Bonnard* and the Anatole France of *Thaïs*. What
had happened in the ten intervening years? What
new experience had been his? Whatever the nature
of that experience, it seems moderately certain
that it would have made a marked, but perhaps not
altogether favourable impression on the worthy
Monsieur Bonnard. What the critics call his "sen-
sualisme" had made unmistakable progress. His
appreciation of Beauty, "which assails with sweet
unrest the souls of those who would fain lay bare
her mystery," had taken a far more definite and
concrete form. He had almost certainly stepped

on a mandragora, which, as we learn from the
Rôtisserie de la Reine Pédauque, is even more terrible
than to drink a love-philtre. Are we to suppose
that he was merely giving play to the imagination—
the detached impersonal imagination of the artist—
when he put this desperate cry of love and anguish
into the mouth of Paphnutius?

" Fool, fool, that I was not to have possessed
Thaïs while there was yet time! Fool, to have
believed that there was anything else in the world
but her! Oh, madness! I dreamed of God, of
the salvation of my soul, of life eternal—as if all
that counted for anything when I had seen Thaïs.
Why did I not feel that blessed eternity was in a
single kiss of that woman, and that, without her,
life was senseless and no more than an evil dream.
. . . She opened to thee her arms—flesh mingled
with the perfume of flowers—and thou wast not
engulfed in the unspeakable enchantments of her
unveiled breast . . . light of day, silvery shadows
of night stars, heavens, trees with trembling crests,
savage beasts, domestic animals, all the anxious
souls of men, do you not hear? ' Thaïs is dying!'
Disappear, ye lights, breezes, and perfumes! Hide
yourselves, ye shapes and thoughts of the universe!
' Thaïs is dying!' She was the beauty of the world,
and all that drew near to her grew fair in the reflection of her grace."

The man who wrote that must himself have had experience of that overmastering passion of which he had read long ago when, as a boy, he read the *Antigone* in the street on his way home from school

Ἔρως ἀνίκατε μάχαν,
Ἔρως, ὃς ἐν κτήμασι πίπτεις

It implies no ordinary pedestrian, domestic affection; but that irresistible passion that whirls away its victims like a leaf driven before the wind :

C'est Vénus tout entière à sa proie attachée.

But if, now, the *Mater Sæva Cupidinum* had made him her victim, he, as we may gather from the two succeeding novels, was, like Horace, to suffer the inevitable shipwreck, and in due course we shall find him, like Horace, hanging up his votive tablet and his dripping garments in honour of the stern god of the sea : the luring, treacherous, hungry sea which is Woman and the passion she inspires.

Though the intervening years had witnessed the appearance of a volume of short stories, *Mother of Pearl*, of which we shall speak in another place, it was not until three years later, in 1893, that Anatole France published his next novel *At the Sign of the Reine Pédauque.* " It marks," says Mr. W. J. Locke of *The Reine Pédauque*, " the flood tide of his genius, when his imaginative power at its brightest came into conjunction with the full ripeness of his scholarship." Another critic, Mr. Robert Blatchford, has spoken of it in terms of still more enthusiastic praise : " The great scene of the banquet in the house of Monsieur de la Guéritaude," says he, " is one of the most artistic, humorous, human and exhilarating things in literature. . . . There is nothing finer or stronger in the best comedy work of Shakespeare." Matthew Arnold, speaking about Lord Macaulay, said, " he has his own heightened and telling way of putting things, and we must always make allowance for it." Perhaps we may say the same of Mr. Blatchford. The Editor of *The Clarion* is a sort of Tartarin of literature, and he sees everything magnified and intensified in the rays of his own glowing enthusiasms. And then, again, the Abbé Jérôme Coignard has for critics reared in the later Victorian traditions this overwhelming asset : he is decidedly not respectable. What an immense relief to escape from the chill decorum and rigid conventionality of Victorian society into the amazing company of this learned and licentious Abbé. If we must see life steadily, it is equally important to see it whole, and there is nothing hidden or slurred over in *The Reine Pédauque*. Jérôme Coignard, with some of his companions, notably Frère Ange, seems to have been borrowed from *Le Conte de Gabalis* by the Abbé Montfaucon de Villars, and from *Le Compère*

Mathieu by Canon Dulaurens. Monsieur Jean Émile Morel rather testily points out the resemblances between the characters and situations in these works and the *Reine Pédauque*. They are striking, they are indeed *pièces à conviction*, but they convict Monsieur France not of plagiarism, but of genius. They are at once as similar and as dissimilar as Shakespeare's lines beginning :

" Ye elves of hills, brooks, standing lakes, and grooves "

and the passage from Golding's translation of Ovid's *Metamorphoses* beginning :

" Ye Ayres and Windes : ye Elves of Hilles, of Brookes, of Woods alone "

on which they are founded. The industrious and learned Monsieur Morel then deserves our gratitude. His " confrontation " of the *Rôtisserie de la Reine Pédauque* with its sources, or with one of them, has but enhanced the glory of Anatole France, who has breathed upon the ashes and wakened them into life. But to return to Jérôme Coignard. He is just a character invented or, if you will have it so, adapted by Anatole France in order that he may discourse upon whatever topic chance or the humour of the moment may suggest. No mouthpiece was ever more conveniently chosen. The genial Abbé is an irresistibly attractive mixture of saint and sinner, of philosopher and philanderer;

K

wise, but with a fine taste for wine and women. Now, assuming that Anatole France's work is largely autobiographical—and never was assumption better founded—it is quite evident that in the years that intervened between the publication of *Thaïs* and that of the *Reine Pédauque*, his attitude towards woman had undergone a marked change. If *Thaïs* marks the period of passion, the *Reine Pédauque* marks the period of disillusionment; and that the passion and the disillusionment were experienced and not merely imagined is beyond question, and, so far as Monsieur France is concerned, nothing, we think, could be wider of the mark than the notion conveyed by Mr. Locke when he tells us that " there dwells in the heart of the mildest scholar a little demon of unrest whom academies may ·imprison but cannot kill." Another interpreter, Mr. Lewis Piaget Shanks, has taken the same line. " Who," he asks, " can sketch a rascal or a vagabond so well as your cloistered scholar ? " One wonders how Monsieur France regards this portrait of himself : the mild and cloistered scholar having a purely imaginary fling and sowing ghostly wild-oats—in the seclusion of his study. It would not be surprising to learn that he is not particularly flattered. Madame Borély, who brings to the problem all the delicate intuition of her sex, throws a very different light on the matter. " Like

Stendhal," she says, " France has known a great
many women ; like him, he has felt the charm of
their intercourse and experienced all the phases
of attraction : attachment, friendship, affection
and passion. He has not disdained the fairest
fountain of delight. . . . Let there be no mistake,
woman is the object of his predilections."

" Like Stendhal." Well, this is what France himself says about Stendhal : " so far as we can make
out, he was a great lover. Wife or maid, town-bred
or country-bred, naught in the shape of a woman
was too hot or too cold for him. And he had a
particular predilection for hotel serving-maids."
It was Oscar Wilde, was it not, who remarked how
difficult it was to divest oneself of a good reputation.
The " cloistered scholar " legend—for which, of
course, Monsieur Sylvestre Bonnard is responsible—
dies hard, but if *Thaïs* and the *Reine Pédauque* left
anything to be done in this direction, his next novel
in order of date, *The Red Lily*—for *The Opinions
of Monsieur Jérôme Coignard* are but a compendium
of philosophical reflections by that engaging personage, a sort of overflow from the *Reine Pédauque*—
ought to have accomplished it.

The Red Lily is more conventional in treatment
than any other of Anatole France's novels. It is
a study of love and jealousy, and a masterly one.
In no other work of modern times has the passion

of jealousy, its terrible and irremediable nature, been delineated with such pitiless and convincing psychological insight. Thérèse Martin-Bellême, the daughter of a rich financier, had made a loveless marriage, a marriage of convenience. There was no sort of bond, save the legal one, betwixt her husband and herself. Before long they drifted asunder, as was inevitable. Their separation, we are told, had been frank and complete. And since then, strangers the one to the other, they had both been grateful for their mutual deliverance. Two years later, Thérèse became the mistress of Robert Le Ménil, a well-to-do bachelor, a man of fashion, a sportsman and a good fellow. She gave herself to him " because he loved her." She had the satisfaction of knowing herself loved, but not the deeper joy of loving. That was to come. Thérèse is invited to Florence to spend a few weeks with an old friend, a Miss Bell, an Englishwoman of cultured tastes and a poetess, who is presented to us as something of an oddity. Wealthy and good-natured, Miss Bell loves to surround herself with persons of talent and genius, artists, poets, musicians, dilettanti. Into this company the fates bring Dechartre, a highly gifted sculptor, a man of refined yet passionate nature, whose bare acquaintance Thérèse had made just before she left Paris on her Italian visit. Thrown together in the home of

Miss Bell, they conceive a mutual attachment which soon ripens on both sides into passionate love. Lightly, thoughtlessly, not reflecting what she did, she had encouraged him. Swiftly, without warning, Love takes its revenge, and they realize when it is too late that they are entangled irrevocably in its toils. Struggling, she knew in her heart how vainly, she proffers him her friendship. He rejects it, fiercely, almost brutally.

She yields at length. The tie that bound her to Le Ménil, whom she had never really loved, was swept away in the torrent of this new and over-mastering passion. They love, this man and woman, hitherto clothed with all the reticences prescribed by a highly artificialized state of society; they love, this artist and this accomplished woman of the world, with all the abandon, the naked ferocity of primitive things. Forgetful of the past, careless of the future, they drink deep of their cup of happiness. Henceforth life has a new, an unimagined significance for them. Le Ménil, her *amant attitré*, who is as deeply in love with Thérèse as his more ordinary and prosaic nature will allow, grows uneasy at her prolonged absence and demands to know the date of her return. She has not the courage or the heart to write him a soothing letter, to put him off with lies and promises. She allows him to guess the truth. In vague terms she accuses herself. She writes mysteriously of souls carried away on the waves of life, and how powerless one is on the ocean of vicissitude. Sadly and tenderly she asks him to keep a kindly memory of her in one corner of his heart. This letter had the obvious and inevitable effect. It brought Le Ménil post haste to Florence. She sees him in a room in his hotel. She tells him, or rather suffers him to guess, that she has another lover; that it is all over between them. Le Ménil breaks out into a torrent of reproaches. In his blind fury he even strikes her. Nevertheless when he writes, " I leave to-morrow evening at seven. Be at the station," she obeys the peremptory summons. That visit to the station marks the beginning of the end. Dechartre learns from some innocent observations of the garrulous Miss Bell that Thérèse has been seen at the station talking to some one, a man, obviously a Parisian. Though for the moment by her protests and assurances she averts the crisis, yet it is to come. The scene is now changed to Paris. There the lovers renew again the joys and raptures that had been theirs at Florence. Then comes a separation : Thérèse has to go away with her family to Dinard. There Dechartre writes to her and unburdens his heart. Since he had loved her, he said, his feet had moved so lightly and so swiftly that they had hardly touched the ground. He had only one fear, and that was that

he was dreaming and should awake to find he did
not know her. Yes, he must be dreaming. But
what a dream! The little house in the Via Alfieri,
the inn at Meudon! Their kisses, and those divine
shoulders, that supple form, fresh and fragrant
as a stream flowing among flowers. Then came
another letter immediately following the first:
" Thérèse, Thérèse," he writes now, " why were
you ever mine if you could not give your whole
self? Your deception has done me no good, since
now I know what I was determined not to know."

What was the cause of this sudden change of
mood? He tells her. As he was lunching at a
tavern in the Rue Royale, he met an old friend,
who was passing through Paris on his way from an
inland watering-place to the seaside. They began
to talk; and it chanced that this man, who moved
much in society, spoke of Thérèse, whom he knew.
He made allusion to the affair with Le Ménil, adding
that the story was common property. On all
this Dechartre puts the worst construction. His
jealousy is in full blaze again. He imagines that
all the time she was receiving his caresses she was
still keeping up her liaison with Le Ménil. " Your
meeting at the railway station in Florence," he
wrote, " should have told me, if only I had not so
obstinately clung to my illusions, in spite of evidence.
I refused to know you were another's, when you

were giving yourself to me with that bold grace, that charming voluptuousness, the thought of which will kill me. I willingly remained in ignorance. I ceased to ask you for an explanation out of fear lest you should find yourself unable to lie. . . . Oh! how I wish I could forget you and everything. But I cannot. You know that you alone can make me forget you. I am always seeing you with him. It is torture. That night on the Arno's bank I thought myself unhappy. But then I did not even know what suffering meant. To-day," he added bitterly, " I know."

Thérèse finds some pretext for leaving her friends, and hurries away, at the earliest opportunity, to Paris. She reassures him once more and banishes his fears, apparently for ever. They were never so happy. The days went by on golden wings. It is an instance of tragic irony. The supreme and irrevocable parting is at hand. Le Ménil reappears on the scene. He makes one last despairing appeal, at the Opera one evening when she was there with a company of friends. When the performance was over, he contrived to help her on with her cloak. On to her bare shoulders, touching them lightly with his fingers, he put the great cloak of red velvet embroidered with gold and lined with ermine, and said in a low voice, very briefly and very distinctly :

" Thérèse, I love you. Remember what I asked you the day before yesterday. Every day, every day, after three o'clock, I shall be in our flat in the Rue Spontini."

At that moment, as she bent her head for him to put on her cloak, she saw Dechartre, with his hand on the door-handle. He looked at her with all the reproach and sorrow the human eye is capable of expressing. Then he turned away down the corridor. It was as if hammers of fire were beating on the walls of her heart, and she remained motionless on the threshold.

There is one more scene between the lovers— a scene of pleading and vain explanation on the part of Thérèse, of blank, inexorable wrath, alternating with sorrow and despair, on that of Dechartre. " I don't believe you! I don't believe you! " he reiterated brutally to all her protestations. The pathos and tragedy of the end are almost unbearable.

" . . . in the passion of her rejected love, she threw herself into his arms and covered him with tears and kisses.

" He forgot everything, took her, aching, broken, but happy, and pressed her in his arms with the mournful rage of desire. Already, her head thrown back on the pillow, she was smiling through her tears. Suddenly he tore himself away from her.

" ' I no longer see you alone. The other is always with you.' "

" Silent, indignant, despairing, she looked at him. She rose, arranged her dress and her hair, with a feeling of shame that was new to her. Then, realizing that the end had come, she looked around her in astonishment, with eyes that saw nothing, and went out slowly."

Such is the theme of *The Red Lily*. It is, as we have said, an analysis of the passion of jealousy. It lays bare, as with a scalpel, the morbidity, the sombre ferocity, the meanness, the pitiable and pathetic helplessness of those stricken with this malignant malady of heart and brain. It shows how the perceptions are quickened by it, as by some potent and maleficent drug, to such preternatural acuteness, that not a word, not a gesture passes unobserved and unsuspected. Let there be but an unfamiliar inflexion in the voice, the slightest hesitation or embarrassment of demeanour, a whisper, a glance, and behold the poor frenzied mind is sent helplessly reeling, clutching wildly as it tosses hither and thither at any motive that may serve to explain the suspicious phenomenon. The passions, Anatole France somewhere observes, are all irrational. But none is so irrational as jealousy, for it inevitably precipitates the crisis of which it stands perpetually in terror. The jealous man knows this, yet he is utterly powerless to control his thoughts or his words. There is but one hope for him. His imagination lashed to the point of madness by the remorseless furies of jealousy, shall only recover its sanity and its poise if he refuses to dwell on the object of his anguish. From that once beloved object he must resolutely avert his gaze. The decree must be absolute and irrevocable. There is, as Dechartre knew, no other way. "She went out slowly." *He did not call her back.*

CHAPTER X

THE NOVELIST

II

Y many *The Gods are Athirst* is held to be France's crowning achievement in fiction. It certainly stands high in the ranks of the historical novel. Few writers have been so well qualified, whether in respect of knowledge or sympathy, to treat of the French Revolution as Anatole France. From his youth upwards he has made the period a subject of special study. When to the re-creation of a highly dramatic series of events in history is brought knowledge accurate and profound, illumined by a rich and sympathetic imagination, the result is very likely to be a masterpiece. That *The Gods are Athirst* deserves this appellation few would deny. Nevertheless, it would not be surprising to learn that many find it more admirable than engaging. It is, of course, absurd, and not to be justified by any canons of criticism, to assess the value of a novel according to the attractiveness of the characters it portrays. But human nature—

and even some critics fall into that category—is
often irrational, and in the long run, despite its
undoubted power, we may not unreasonably wonder
whether it will be numbered among those works
by which Anatole France will chiefly retain his
hold on the gratitude and affection of posterity.
The men and women it portrays are, for the most
part, so cruel or so mean, so disloyal or so selfish,
that one recoils, as in incredulous horror or disgust,
from what seems a hideous travesty of human
nature. Of all the characters in the book, only
Brotteaux, a *ci-devant* farmer of taxes now reduced
to cutting out dancing dolls in cardboard, Louis
de Longuemare, a monk driven from his cloister,
and Marthe, who called herself Athenaïs, a pretty
little Magdalen, engage our sympathies. The hero
of the story is Évariste Gamelin, a young painter
who was inspired by the cold and lofty classicism
of David. He lives in a garret with his old mother.
His sister, a beautiful girl, has earned his eternal
hatred by fleeing the country with a royalist lover.
Through the influence of a wealthy woman of easy
virtue, who had looked with desire upon the pale
handsome features and slim graceful figure of this
ascetic young man, the possessor of a beauty at once
austere and feminine, the countenance of a Minerva,
he is made a member of the Revolutionary Tribunal
and eventually himself dies beneath the guillotine

to which he had helped to devote so many victims. Évariste Gamelin is not a heartless man. On the contrary, he is capable of high and generous impulses, of deeds of self-sacrifice. He is one of those stern but narrow idealists, one of those dangerous doctrinaire enthusiasts, of whom Robespierre is the typical example, and whose very sincerity, whose incorruptible fervour lead them to perpetrate, with icy and unshakeable resolution, deeds of unutterable cruelty. To quote the words in which Gamelin describes the crime of Orestes, whom he had begun to portray on canvas, " he was driven by a sacred obligation to commit his dreadful deed—a sin the gods cannot but pardon, but which men will never condone. To avenge outraged justice he repudiated Nature, made himself a monster, tore out his own heart." Évariste Gamelin, to whom these words are singularly applicable, is a striking exception to what we have elsewhere said about the static nature of Monsieur France's character. He *does* develop under the influence of events, and with a vengeance. He who went without bread rather than that a complete stranger to him should lack her ration, and had then—*splendide mendax*—deceived his mother by telling her he had eaten his portion on the way back in order that she might take her own share without misgiving, this same man, before the end of the story, is ready, with hardly a tremor, to send his own sister to her doom. The scene in question is one of terrible intensity. Julie—the sister—has returned with her royalist lover to France. The lover is arrested and condemned to death. Julie, disguised as a man, comes to the garret where her mother and her brother Évariste have their lodgings, to implore the latter to intercede for her lover on the Tribunal. Évariste is out, and the mother and daughter hold a hurried and anxious colloquy.

" Suddenly "—so the narrative runs—" with a keenness of hearing sharpened by anxiety, she caught the sound of her son's step on the stairs.

" ' Évariste,' she cried. ' Hide '—and she hurried the girl into the bedroom.

" ' How are you to-day, mother dear ? '

" Évariste hung up his hat on its peg, changed his blue coat for a working jacket, and sat down before his easel.

" ' Évariste ! '

" ' Mother ? '

" ' I have had news . . . guess of whom. . . .'

" ' I do not know.'

" ' Of Julie . . . of your sister. . . . She is not happy.'

" ' It would be a scandal if she were.'

" ' Do not speak so, my son, she is your sister. Julie is not a bad woman ; she had a good disposition,

which misfortune has developed. She loves you.
I can assure you, Évariste, that she only desires a
hard-working, exemplary life, and her fondest wish
is to be reconciled to her friends. There is nothing
to prevent your seeing her again. She has married
Fortuné Chassagne.'

" ' She has written to you ? "

" ' No.'

" ' How, then, have you had news of her,
mother ? '

" ' It was not by letter, Évariste; it was . . .'

" He sprang up and stopped her with a savage
cry :

" ' Not another word, mother ! Do not tell
me they have both returned to France. . . . As
they are doomed to perish, at least let it not be at
my hands. For their own sake, for yours, for mine,
let me not know they are in Paris. . . . Do not
force the knowledge on me, otherwise . . .'

" ' What do you mean, my son ? You would
think, you would dare . . . ? '

" ' Mother, hear what I say; if I knew my sister
Julie to be in that room . . .' (and he pointed to
the closed door), ' I should go instantly to denounce
her to the Committee of Vigilance of the Section.'

" The poor mother, her face as white as her coif,
dropped her knitting from her trembling hands and
sighed in a voice fainter than the faintest whisper :

" ' I would not believe it, but I see it now; my boy is a monster . . .' "

There is a love story running through the book, the love of Évariste Gamelin and Élodie Blaise, the daughter of a picture-dealer. This is how she sealed her hard-won victory over the pale, ascetic young idealist.

" They went to the Amour Peintre " (her father's shop).

" ' Better not go through the shop,' Élodie suggested. She made him go in by the main coach-door and mount the stairs with her to the suite of rooms above. On the landing she drew out of her reticule a heavy iron key.

" ' It might be the key of a prison,' she exclaimed. ' Évariste, you are going to be my prisoner.'

" They crossed the dining-room and were in the girl's bedchamber.

" Évariste felt upon his the ardent freshness of Élodie's lips. He pressed her in his arms; with her head thrown back and swooning eyes, her hair flowing loose over her relaxed form, half-fainting, she escaped his hold and ran to shoot the bolt. . . .

" The night was far advanced when citoyenne Blaise opened the outer door of the flat for her lover, and whispered to him in the darkness :

" ' Good-bye, sweetheart ! it is the hour my father

L

will be coming home. If you hear a noise on the stairs, go up quick to the higher floor and don't come down till all danger is over of your being seen. To have the street-door opened, give three raps on the concierge's window. Good-bye, my life, good-bye, my soul ! '

" When he found himself in the street he saw the window of Élodie's chamber half unclose and a little hand pluck a red carnation, which fell at his feet like a drop of blood."

Élodie is his Nirvana. Alone within her sheltering arms does he seek and find peace and forgetfulness from the legions of hideous thoughts that beset his tormented brain. . . .

At last he himself is passing in the tumbril to the place of execution.

" As the cart passed in front of the window of the blue chamber, a woman's hand, wearing a silver ring on the ring-finger, pushed aside the edge of the blind and threw towards Gamelin a red carnation, which his bound hands prevented him from catching, but which he adored as the token and likeness of those red and fragrant lips that had refreshed his mouth. His eyes filled with blinding tears, and his whole being was entranced with the glamour of this farewell when he saw the blood-stained knife rise into view in the Place de la Révolution."

Gamelin is executed. A month or two passes. There is another love scene.

Desmahis, an artist, a former friend of Gamelin's, accompanies Élodie in a cabriolet to her father's house.

" ' Good-bye,' said Élodie, jumping out of the cabriolet.

" But Desmahis begged so hard, he was so tenderly urgent and spoke so sweetly that she had not the heart to leave him at the door.

" ' It is late,' she said; ' you must only stay an instant.'

" In the blue chamber she threw off her mantle and appeared in her white gown *a l'antique*, which displayed all the warm fullness of her shape.

" ' You are cold perhaps,' she said. ' I will light the fire; it is already laid.'

" She struck the flint and put a lighted match to the fire.

" Philippe took her in his arms with the gentleness which bespeaks strength, and she felt a strange delicious thrill. She was already yielding beneath his kisses when she snatched herself from his arms, crying :

" ' Let me be.'

" Slowly she uncoiled her hair before the chimney-glass; then she looked mournfully at the ring she wore on the ring-finger of her left hand, a little silver ring on which the face of Marat, all worn and battered, could no longer be made out. She looked at it till the tears confused her sight, took it off softly and tossed it into the flames.

" Then, her face shining with tears and smiles, transfigured with tenderness and passion, she threw herself into Philippe's arms.

" The night was far advanced when the citoyenne Blaise opened the outer door of the flat for her lover and whispered to him in the darkness :

" ' *Good-bye, sweetheart. It is the hour when my father will be coming home. If you hear a noise on the stairs, go up quick to the higher floor and don't come down till all danger is over of your being seen. To have the street-door opened, give three raps on the concierge's window. Good-bye, my life, good-bye, my soul !* '

" The last dying embers were glowing on the hearth when Élodie, tired and happy, dropped her head on her pillow."

Mightier in its irony than the most eloquent indictment, the bitterest denunciation, is that simple expedient of making her repeat word for word, in parting from Desmahis, the phrases with which she had dismissed Gamelin on the night when first they came to the fulfilment of their desires.

We are told that those struggles which loom so great in the history of England, the Wars of the

Roses, the conflict of Cavalier and Roundhead, had but little effect on the habits of the great mass of the population. Life went on pretty much as usual. The fields were tilled and sown, and the harvests gathered in, and the craftsmen did not cease their labours. And in this story, though our attention is focussed on the sinister activities of the Revolutionary Tribunal, though the grim shadow of the guillotine broods perpetually over the scene, though the air is unquiet with tidings of conflict and disaster, nevertheless, in order to correct the impression of universal tragedy that all this might convey, the curtain of war is lifted now and again, and we are suffered to behold the stream of life flowing on its familiar course—men going about their ordinary avocations, women working, love-making, gossiping, talking about dress unwitting or heedless of the history that is being made around them. Even the names of the great protagonists, names that ring out with such tragic distinctness across the gulf of years were, then, often devoid of significance for the masses. To impress this upon us, Monsieur France employs the same ironic device which he used with such memorable effect in the *Procurator of Judea*. Évariste Gamelin having learned with horror of the assassination of Marat, was on his way, his heart bursting with grief and hate and love, to pay a last mark of respect

to the martyr of liberty. As he is pushing his
way through the excited throng, an old country-
woman, wearing the coif of the Limousin peasantry,
accosts him to ask *if the Monsieur Marat who had
been murdered was Monsieur le Curé Mara of Saint-
Pierre-de-Quesnoix !*

In this tragedy the chorus is supplied by Monsieur
Brotteaux des Ilettes. He, of course, is none other
than Monsieur France himself in the guise of an
ex-farmer of taxes, who had now exchanged the
luxurious refinement which had been his under the
monarchy, for the misery and squalor of a garret.
Notwithstanding the misfortunes which had come
upon him, his philosophic calm was undisturbed,
his soul was not embittered, his cheerfulness did
not desert him even at the point of death. Brotteaux, Père Longuemare the Barnabite monk,
and Athenaïs the little harlot, are conveyed to the
guillotine in the same tumbril.

" ' Sir,' said Père Longuemare to the Epicurean
philosopher, ' I ask you a favour ; this God in whom
you do not yet believe, pray to Him for me. It
is far from sure that you are not nearer to Him
than I am myself ; a moment can decide this. A
second, and you may be called by the Lord to be
His highly favoured son. Sir, pray for me.'

" While the wheels were grinding over the pave-
ment of the long Faubourg Antoine, the monk

A GROUP AT LA BÉCHELLERIE

Anatole France, Lucien Psichari, Mme France and a Friend
From a photograph by M. Henry Davray

was busy, with heart and lips, reciting the prayers of
the dying. Brotteaux's mind was fixed on reading
the lines of the poet of nature : *Sic ubi non erimus.*
. . . Bound as he was and shaken in the vile, jolting
cart, he preserved his calm and even showed a certain
solicitude to maintain an easy posture. At his side,
Athenaïs, proud to die like the Queen of France,
surveyed the crowd with haughty looks, and the
old financier, noting as a connoisseur the girl's
white bosom, was filled with regret for the light
of day."

Penguin Island (L'Île des Pingouins) was among
Monsieur France's most popular books. In its
English dress, it has gone through four editions,
and that notwithstanding the fact that it is exclu-
sively a caricature of the history of France, and that
a large part of it consists of an ironic description
of the Dreyfus case. Frankly *Penguin Island*, with
its facile, almost cheap, satire, strikes us now as the
least pleasing of Monsieur France's books, nor does
the skill with which it is written redeem its many
crudities, its frequent lapses from good taste.
Aged, half-blind, but, despite his heavy burden
of years, still filled with missionary zeal, Saint Maël,
a Breton monk, sails away in a stone trough over
the Arctic seas and lands at length on an island
inhabited by a colony of penguins. With his imperfect vision he takes them for the council or parlia-

mentary assembly of the isle seated in solemn
conclave like the *Patres Conscripti* at Rome, or the
Council of the Areopagus at Athens.   He proceeds
to evangelize them with all the eloquence at his
command, and hearing, at the conclusion of his
discourse, what he took to be a confused murmur
of approbation, accompanied, as he dimly perceived,
by sage noddings of the head, he straightway
baptized them.   The scene is now changed to
heaven, and we listen to a long debate on the problem
presented by this well-intentioned but untimely
and preposterous piece of proselytizing zeal.   The
deity at length takes the only course open to him
and changes the penguins to men, endowing them
with human bodies and immortal souls.   The metamorphosis is performed through the agency of Saint
Maël, who was plunged into consternation when he
realized the consequences of his too hasty zeal.
But the penguins now being men and women, the
good monk is seized with the fear that if left to
themselves they may fall away from grace, an
apprehension only too abundantly justified by his
previous experience.   So, setting sail in his marvellous
trough, he tows the island, with its freight of con-
verts, back to the Breton shore, an achievement in
navigation which, being a saint, he accomplished
without difficulty.   From this point their history
as Frenchmen begins.   It would, of course, be a

miracle if the book did not contain much that is diverting, much that is legitimately entertaining, but perhaps it is the very facility of the theme that is its undoing; that causes the irony to degenerate into burlesque and the satire into caricature.

Somewhat akin to *Penguin Island,* but, on the whole, lighter in touch, and more gracious in expression, is the novel which in its earliest form appeared under the title *Les Anges* as a serial in *Gil Blas,* a paper which an old French professor of my acquaintance once roundly described to me as *un journal de cocottes.* If this was an unbiassed description of it, the fair but frail ladies who sucked the somewhat dubious honey of its pages must have found much to suit their taste in *The Revolt of the Angels,* which recounts the adventures in modern Paris of certain angels, who, wearying of the monotony and restraints imposed upon them by their celestial existence, decide to throw off the yoke and to seek distraction in the society of men—and women. Arrived on earth, they disport themselves in a manner that affords a striking contrast with the popularly received notions of angelic existence. As the beautiful Madame des Aubels was not slow to discover from a certain infallible indication which obtruded itself upon her notice when the angel Arcade was assisting her to dress, angels are formed in every respect like men, and are subject to the same desires. Arcade is but one of a whole company of beings who, in heaven, were cherubim and seraphim, and, on earth, are artists, musicians, anarchists, nihilists, living the careless, hand-to-mouth existence that is normal with the inhabitants of Bohemia. These angels, having taken on an earthly form, live the life of ordinary mortals. Istar, for example, had belonged to the choir of Cherubim or Kerûbs who see above them only the Seraphim. He had formerly borne in heaven the bodily shape of a winged bull surmounted by the head of a horned and bearded man. When he stood erect with outspread wings he covered with his shadow sixty archangels. Embodied in human form and reduced to the stature of Adam, he still retained some characteristics of his former nature. His big, protruding eyes, his beaked nose, his thick lips framed in a black beard which descended in curls on to his chest, recalled those cherubs of the tabernacle of Iaveh of which the bulls of Nineveh afford a pretty accurate representation. While, awaiting the coming of the hour when he should deliver heaven from bondage, he dreamed of the salvation of regenerate humanity, and was eager to consummate the destruction of this wicked world in order to raise upon its ashes, to the sound of the lyre, a city radiant with happiness and love. A chemist, in the pay of a dealer in nitrates, he lived very frugally.

He wrote for newspapers with advanced views on liberty, spoke at public meetings, and had got himself sentenced several times to terms of imprisonment for anti-militarism. But it was Arcade, the latest to arrive from the celestial regions, who endeavoured to inspire his brother angels with the spirit of revolt. At length, after divers adventures on this earth, in which they show themselves possessed of all the appetites and passions by which ordinary humanity is animated, the angels decide to seek out Satan and, under his leadership, to join in a new assault upon the crystal battlements of heaven. " Climbing the seven steep terraces which rise up from the bed of the Ganges to the temples muffled in creepers, the five angels reached, by half-obliterated paths, the wild garden filled with perfumed clusters of grapes and chattering monkeys, and, at the far end thereof, they discovered him whom they had come to seek. The archangel lay with his elbow on black cushions embroidered with golden flames. At his feet crouched lions and gazelles. Twined in the trees, tame serpents turned on him their friendly gaze. At the sight of his angelic visitors his face grew melancholy. Long since, in the days when, with his brow crowned with grapes and his sceptre of vine leaves in his hand, he had taught and comforted mankind, his heart had many times been heavy with sorrow ; but never yet, since his glorious downfall, had his beautiful face expressed such pain and anguish."

Satan bids his visitors welcome and gives them refreshment. He bids them slumber pleasantly in the garden. On the morrow, he says, he will give his reply to their prayer that he will lead them in a renewed attack on heaven. Then Satan himself falls asleep and has a vision.

In his dream he sees the fallen angels under his supreme command gathered together in a mighty host armed with the most modern weapons of destruction and led by generals skilled in the science and art of war. Against these new and terrible engines of war, the obsolete thunder of Ialdabaoth is of no avail. ". . . a rain of fire falls on the Mountain of God, Satan's army is not yet in sight, but the walls of topaz, the cupolas of emerald, the roofs of diamond, all fall in with an appalling crash under the discharge of the electrophores. The ancient thunder-clouds essay to reply, but the bolts fall short and their thunders are lost in the deserted plains of the skies. The legions of Satan are victorious. But, alas, nothing is won, nothing is changed. Conquering, he grows hard and cruel as the power he had dispossessed, while the fallen Ialdabaoth becomes just and compassionate. Satan, awaking, bathed in an icy sweat, now gives his answer to the angels who had gathered around him.

" ' Comrades,' he says, ' my answer is, No—
we will not conquer the heavens. Enough to have
the power. War engenders war, and victory defeat.
God, conquered, will become Satan; Satan, conquering, will become God. . . . As to ourselves,
celestial spirits, sublime demons, we have destroyed
Ialdabaoth, our Tyrant, if in ourselves we have
destroyed Ignorance and Fear.' " The words were
prophetic, for six months after they were written,
Europe was plunged in the greatest and most
destructive war in the history of the world, which
has been followed by a " peace " that has reproduced
with unwelcome accuracy the predictions of Satan
—and of Monsieur France.

The Revolt of the Angels contains some passages of
sustained poetic beauty. Few pages that Monsieur
France has written can rival, and none can surpass,
the story of the world's destiny as unfolded by old
Nectaire the Flute-player. Nowhere in the whole
range of Monsieur France's works have irony and
poetry been brought into such startling and incongruous juxtaposition as in this book. To such an
extent is this the case that one almost has the illusion
that it has been written by two distinct hands,
and that no sooner had the poet and dreamer laid
down the pen than it was taken up with mephisto-
phelian glee by the ironist and the mocker. Monsieur France—so he told me—considers that this

book contains some of his best writing, is, in fact, his finest book. Certainly the compiler of a " Wit and Wisdom of Anatole France " would find much to his hand in this volume. Nevertheless, despite its wit and power, it is improbable that posterity will endorse this view.

A sort of " pendant " to *The Red Lily* is *A Mummer's Tale*, under which title has been translated *Histoire Comique*. This book is a study of love and jealousy. An actor is passionately in love with a brilliant and beautiful actress, whose favours he has enjoyed but who has forsaken him for another, a wealthy and handsome young diplomat. The jilted lover pursues his mistress with reproaches, prayers and threats. He follows her, lies in wait for her, spies upon her. At length, having waited, one evening, for the actress and her new lover to leave the house where they had their assignations, he shoots himself in their presence, crying, as he pulls the trigger, " I forbid you to belong to one another. This is my dying wish. Good-bye, Félicie."

From that time forth love, or at all events the accomplishment of the physical act of love, becomes impossible for her. As, in *The Red Lily*, Dechartre, when he was about to fulfil his desires, beheld the image of his supposed rival, with an intolerable and maddening distinctness, so in this book Félicie, whenever her lover essays to take her, sees with hideous clearness the form and features of the suicide, who gazes at her with an expression which sends her into transports of terror. Nothing avails to cure her of this terrible obsession, and at last she realizes in despair that she is irrevocably sundered from the man whom she so passionately desires by the unappeasable spirit of him who had murdered himself for her sake.

There is something at once attractive and repellent about this book. The sordid, selfish people who form the *dramatis personae* move and speak and have their being in a sort of cruel, pitiless glare that brings out into ghastly relief all the ugliness of their starved souls, so that one gets the impression of looking at a play too close to the footlights. Alone among them all Dr. Trublet—Dr. Socrates, as he is familiarly called—the official medical adviser to the theatre and the familiar friend and confidant of the actors and actresses, engages our sympathies ; he alone redeems the gaunt, stark ugliness of this story of sordid intrigue. Wise, ironic, compassionate, he sits among his flock, like a good-tempered, easy-going Sultan, scattering, with cynical indolence, his pearls of somewhat mundane wisdom. It seems that, in the green-room, conversation is unhampered by those conventions of reticence which are the accepted rule in less artistic circles.

" ' Doctor,' said Félicie, the ' heroine ' of the story, who had been describing her symptoms with what in a less emancipated society might have been regarded as a somewhat embarrassing minuteness, " ' I want to ask you a question which you may possibly think a droll one; but I do really want to know whether, considering that you know just what there is in the human body, and that you have seen all the things we have inside us, it doesn't embarrass you, at certain moments, in your dealings with women? It seems to me that the idea of all that must disgust you?'

" From the depths of his cushions Trublet, wafting a kiss to Félicie, replied :

" ' My dear child, there is no more exquisitely delicate, rich and beautiful tissue than the skin of a pretty woman. That is what I was telling myself just now, while contemplating the back of your neck, and you will readily understand that, under such an impression——'

" She made a grimace at him like that of a disdainful monkey.

" ' You think it witty, I suppose, to talk nonsense when anyone asks you a serious question?'

" ' Well, then, since you wish it, mademoiselle, you shall have an instructive answer. Some twenty years ago we had, in the post-mortem room at the Hôpital Saint-Joseph, a drunken old watchman named Daddy Rousseau, who every day at eleven o'clock used to lunch at the end of the table on which the corpse was lying. He ate his lunch because he was hungry. Nothing prevents people who are hungry from eating as soon as they have got something to eat. Only Daddy Rousseau used to say: "I don't know whether it is because of the atmosphere of the room, but I must have something fresh and appetizing." '

" Félicie was not slow to seize the meaning of this parable.

" 'I understand,' she said, without a trace of embarrassment; 'little flower-girls are what you want. But you mustn't, you know. And there you are, seated like a Turk, and you haven't written out my prescription yet.' "

Dr. Trublet—who is, of course, one of the many incarnations of Monsieur France himself—is, it cannot be denied, a fascinating personality, and the worst that can be said of him is that he takes somewhat over-kindly to the third-rate company in which his lot is cast. They strike one as third-rate, not indeed because they are immoral—Manon Lescaut was immoral, or, if you will, amoral, yet she is one of the most lovable characters in literature —but because they are all stamped with an irremediable selfishness of soul, and selfishness, in the long run, is almost synonymous with vulgarity.

M

But Dr. Trublet, who had long since " graduated in human nature," is irresistible. He is a cynic, but his cynicism is of the head only, it has not spoilt his heart. " I am," he says, " a medical man. I deal in illusions. I relieve, I console. How is it possible to relieve and console without lying? Only women and physicians know how necessary untruthfulness is, and how beneficial to man."

As for morality, that, according to Dr. Trublet, " is a mutual agreement to keep what we possess : land, houses, furniture, women, and our lives. . . . Every material change produces a moral change, since morals depend upon environment. . . . Why should not humanity succeed in changing nature to the extent of making it pacific? Why should not humanity abolish the law of murder? . . . This world is perhaps irremediably wicked. At all events, I shall have got plenty of amusement out of it. It affords those who are in it an interesting spectacle. . . ." So speaks Trublet of the possibilities of the future, of what mankind may achieve, " miserably puny though it be." Yet never was there a more thorough-going determinist than Trublet. " Since," he says, " we perceive phenomena successively, we actually believe that they follow one another. But it is possible to conceive beings built in such a fashion that they perceive simultaneously what we regard as past and

future. The universe is constructed inevitably a
a triangle of which two angles and one side are given.
Future things are determined."   Or, as Sir Thomas
Browne has it, " the last Trump is already sounded,
the reprobates in the flame, and the blessed in Abra-
ham's bosom."   As for human knowledge, he bids
us found no soaring hopes on that.   " Men were
not made to know," he warns us, " men were not
made to understand. They do not possess the
necessary faculties. A man's brain is larger and
richer in convolutions than that of a gorilla, but
there is no essential difference between the two.
Our highest thoughts and our most comprehensive
systems will never be anything more than the magnificent extension of the ideas contained in the head
of a monkey. We know more about the world than
the dog does, and this flatters and entertains us;
but it is very little in itself, and our illusions increase
with our knowledge."

CHAPTER XI

THE SHORT STORY TELLER

" HAT a superiority, in point of taste, does the short story exhibit in comparison with the novel. How much more delicate it is, more discreet and more certain in its appeal to people with active minds, people whose lives are fully occupied and who know the value of their time. Is not brevity the primary courtesy that a writer owes to his readers? The short story suffices for every need; and, in it, a great deal may be conveyed in a few words. A well-turned tale is a feast for connoisseurs, and a satisfaction to the critical. It is, of fiction, the elixir, the quintessence, the precious ointment."

So writes Monsieur Anatole France, and it is true, at least in his case, that some of his finest work is given to us in the form of the short story. His genius is indeed episodic rather than epic, and in a sense, with perhaps one or two exceptions, all his imaginative writings might be classed, without any violent straining of the definition, as so many short stories.   What are *My Friend's Book*, *Pierre Nozière*, *Little Pierre* and *The Bloom of Life*, but a collection of little stories, exquisite vignettes, strung upon the golden thread of memory?   *The Crime of Sylvestre Bonnard*, as we have seen, consists of two independent tales designed to illustrate the character of that amiable old scholar.   The four volumes of *Histoire Contemporaine* are but a chain of episodes, a chain divided into four sections, each of which terminates for no other apparent reason than that the number of words requisite to complete a volume has been compassed.   The genius of Monsieur France leans towards the small perfect thing.   As someone has said, he is by nature much more of a miniaturist than a painter of frescoes.   The sustained flight is not for him.   Rather does he resemble the bee, passing from flower to flower and distilling honey as least as sweet and delicate as any that Hybla or Hymettus ever gave.

But if Monsieur France is much given to the short story, it is important to bear in mind that he is not content with the mere telling of a tale.   He is not a mere recorder of incidents.   The incident, when there is any, and that is not always, is not the principal part, is not the prime object of the tale.   The main interest is always, or nearly always, a philosophic one.   Take, for example, the famous *Procurator of Judea*.   The " incident " in this tale is merely this. Ælius Lamia, a wealthy and cultured Roman, had been sent into exile by Tiberius because he had had criminal relations with the wife of Sulpicius Quirinus, a man of consular rank. During his eighteen years of exile he travelled all over Syria, Palestine, Cappadocia and Armenia, and made prolonged visits to Antioch, Cæsarea and Jerusalem. At length he was able to return to Rome, where he was permitted to resume a part of his possessions, and where he lived a secluded life in his house on the Esquiline reading the poets and the philosophers. In the sixty-second year of his age, being afflicted with a troublesome ailment, he betook himself to Baiæ, the resort of the pleasure-hunter and the wealthy valetudinarian. There he happens to fall in with Pontius Pilate, with whom he had, in his years of exile, been on terms of closest friendship. Pontius Pilate invites him to supper at his villa, and the two fall to talking over old times. The conversation happens to turn upon the Jews, and Pilate enlarges on the difficulties he has had in dealing with that race of troublesome and ignorant fanatics. Lamia, who still retains the tastes and sympathies of the voluptuary, called to mind a beautiful young Jewess with whom he had fallen deeply in love. " Her loins arched, her head thrown back, and, as it were, dragged down by the weight of her heavy red hair, her eyes swimming with

voluptuousness, eager, languishing, compliant, she
would have made Cleopatra herself grow pale with
envy.   I was in love with her barbaric dances, her
voice—a little raucous and yet so sweet—her
atmosphere of incense, the semi-somnolescent state
in which she seemed to live.   I followed her every-
where.   I mixed with the vile rabble of soldiers,
conjurers and extortioners with which she was
surrounded.   One day, however, she disappeared,
and I saw her no more.   Long did I seek her in
disreputable alleys and taverns.   It was more
difficult to learn to do without her than to lose the
taste for Greek wine.   Some months after I lost sight
of her, I learned by chance that she had attached
herself to a small company of men and women
who were followers of a young Galilean thauma-
turgist.   His name was Jesus : he came from
Nazareth, and he was crucified for some crime, I
don't quite know what.   Pontius, do you remember
anything about the man ? "

Pontius Pilate contracted his brows, and his hand
rose to his forehead in the attitude of one who
probes the deeps of memory.   Then, after a silence
of some seconds :

" Jesus ? " he murmured, " Jesus of Nazareth ?
I cannot call him to mind."

That is the story, and it is wrought with the
exquisite finish of a cameo, which is written with the

design of showing how insignificant an event, not only to the contemporary world, but even to those who had played a prominent part in it, had been the trial and death of Jesus. This little story, for all its slightness, sums up a whole philosophy of history.

Again, no less philosophical in purpose is the story which gives its title to the volume *Balthasar*, which tells how the King of Ethiopia fell in love with the Queen of Sheba, and recounts the adventures which befell them as they wandered by night in the Queen's capital. We learn how the Queen gave him of her love, how she afterwards forsook him for another, how and why she was fain to seek his love again. We are told, too, wherefore Balthasar built an observatory, and what led him to say " the sciences are useful; they keep us from thinking." Purely philosophical, but no less engaging, are the stories in *The White Stone*, which tells how a group of Frenchmen meet together in the Roman Forum and discuss many topics, archæological and historical. One of the company reads a story, of which he is the author, and which describes an event in the official career of the proconsul Gallio in the days of the Emperor Claudius. The story, which introduces St. Paul, is suggested by the incidents referred to in Chapter XVIII of the Acts, and in ironic subtlety and grace of style recalls the Procurator of Judea.

ANATOLE FRANCE IN HIS STUDY

From an original painting by Auguste Leroux, engraved by Ernest Florian.
By permission of M. René Hellen

After *The Procurator of Judea* perhaps the best known of Anatole France's shorter stories is the famous *Crainquebille*, which, as everybody knows, tells how a certain costermonger gets himself clapped into prison on a charge of having said " Mort aux Vaches ! " (Down with the slops) to a policeman. The charge was a false one.   Crainquebille did not use the offensive expression.   But, nevertheless, he was put into gaol.   When he came out he found his custom gone.   No one would have any further dealings with him.   He sank lower and lower in the slough of misery and want, till, worn out with cold, hunger and fatigue, homeless and hopeless, he realized that he would be better off in prison. He therefore went up to a policeman and shouted " Mort aux Vaches ! "   But the policeman was a great-hearted and compassionate man.   He refused to arrest him, and poor Crainquebille " moves on " into the darkness to wander we know not whither. This same volume contains the history of *Putois*, the notorious odd-job man, who never existed, and the thoughts of *Riquet* the dog.   Besides these there are the collections entitled *The Merrie Tales of Jacques Tournebroche*—not to be told *virginibus puerisque*—*Clio*, *The Seven Wives of Bluebeard*. Many of these stories are masterpieces, none of them but will pay richly for the reading.   Wit, humour, fantasy, learning rich and curious, and a profound insight into human nature, such are some of the qualities that entitle their author to be considered a master in a branch of literature which has nowhere been brought to a higher degree of perfection than in France.

CHAPTER XII

THE HISTORIAN

ANY years ago, when I was living in a big provincial city in France, we used to go from time to time to an entertainment known as a *Revue*, which had little or nothing in common with those elaborate and, sometimes, rather meaningless performances that pass under the same name in London to-day.

The *Revue*, as we then knew it, was a sort of rough-and-ready satire on local persons and events, and would consequently have afforded but little interest to those unacquainted with the city in question, its personages and their doings. If, for example, there was anything amiss with any of the public services, the post office, the railway, or what not, the officials would be held up to scorn or ridicule in effective if rather crude burlesque. These *Revues*, in short, consisted of a sort of running ironic commentary on local affairs and people. If for the stage we substitute the pages of a periodical, and, for purely local affairs, the affairs of the nation as a whole, we shall gain a fairly accurate notion of the nature and scope of the four " novels " included under the general title of " Histoire Contemporaine." The central figure of these chronicles or satires, Monsieur Bergeret, is one of Anatole France's great creations, ranking with Sylvestre Bonnard, the Abbé Jérôme Coignard, Monsieur Brotteaux des Ilettes and Doctor Trublet. All classes, from the highest to the lowest, pass in ironic procession through these pages : clerics intriguing for a vacant bishopric, politicians plotting for promotion, fashionable women bartering their favours to secure social advancement for themselves or political advancement for their husbands. Monsieur Bergeret, who is *Maître de Conférences* at a provincial university, is first introduced to us in Chapter VII of *The Elm Tree on the Mall*. " Bergeret was not a happy man, for he had an acute mind whose barbs were not always turned outwards, and very often he pricked himself with the needle-points of his own criticism. He was not popular with his superiors at the University, and, while his scientific and mathematical colleagues gave their lectures in handsome well-lighted rooms, Monsieur Bergeret was obliged to hold forth to a mere handful of students, in a murky, ill-ventilated cellar. His domestic surroundings were still more depressing. He was poor, shut up with his wife and

three daughters in a little dwelling where he tasted
to the full the inconveniences of domestic life,
and it harassed him to find hair-curlers on his writing-
table, and to see the margins of his manuscripts
singed by curling-tongs. The only secure and
pleasant place of retreat that he had in the world
was the bench on the Mall shaded by an ancient
elm, and the secondhand-book corner in Paillot's
shop." But the inconveniences he was compelled
to endure at home and abroad did not impair his
insight into the characters of the people with
whom he was brought into contact. And what
a gallery of portraits is presented to us—Mgr.
Charlot the Cardinal Archbishop, the cautious
but capable administrator, determined to keep in
with the civil authorities; the Abbé Lantaigne,
the Superior of the seminary, so eloquent of speech,
so sturdy in opinion, so downright and uncompromising in his judgments, so jealous a champion
of his Church's rights, and so ill-suited to adjust
himself to the questions and needs of the day:
the much more astute and worldly-wise Abbé
Guitrel, outwardly so liberal, so well-disposed, so
conciliatory towards people of wealth and influence,
but, withal, so resolute and tenacious, showing
himself immovable and adamant when once the
object of his ambitions—the Bishopric of Tour-
coing—was gained, and so making up for the

concessions he had been forced to make to attain it; Loyer, Don Juan and Minister of State; Lacrisse, the Secretary of the " Society of young Royalists "; that vulgar and commonplace Xanthippe, Madame Bergeret; Madame de Bonmont the converted Jewess, who sends her daughter to a fashionable convent school; the beautiful but frail Madame de Gromance; Worms-Clavelin the Prefect, another Jew, vulgar, generous, good-tempered and successful; Zoe, the sister of Monsieur Bergeret, so practical when he is such a dreamer, and lastly, but perhaps most important of all, Riquet, the most delightful dog in fiction.

It necessarily follows, from the form and nature of these books, that many of the matters with which they deal have ceased to have any but a faint and retrospective interest for the present generation. Even the Dreyfus case, so absorbing in its day, has disappeared below the horizon. But if circumstances change, men and women remain pretty much what they have always been, and so long as mankind continues to occupy itself with its " proper study," these essays in contemporary history will never fail to excite our interest.

Critics have not been wanting to animadvert on the " scènes de libertinage " with which these books abound. Some have gone so far as to say that it is this which accounts for the success which they have had abroad. Certainly no writer was ever more skilled than Monsieur Anatole France in saying little and suggesting much. He is a past master in the art of graceful bawdry. " Il y a chez lui," someone has said, " une sensualité ardente, et il ne la dissimule pas. Il a écrit qu'un homme n'est past humain quand il n'est pas sensuel." —" There is about him something ardently sensual— or perhaps we should rather say sensuous—and he does not hide it. He has written that a man is not human when he is not sensual." He is certainly at no pains to hide it, and since he is writing about life as a whole, why should he be? Perhaps the references to Philippe Tricouillard and Hercule Melampyge might have been omitted as being a little out of harmony with modern taste, but all these things are part and parcel of the Anatolian method. It is wise and salutary, thinks Monsieur France, that we should have our noses rubbed occasionally in the common earth.

We have treated these volumes as history rather than fiction, because they do, in fact, offer an example of the historic method, which in the view of Anatole France, we should endeavour to follow. When, in the ordinary way, we look back over the past, we view it in the light of our own knowledge and not at all with the eyes of a contemporary. It is natural and inevitable that we should find it a matter of great difficulty to divest ourselves of the wisdom acquired after the event. When, for example, we study the early history of Christianity, we do so with the knowledge of the stupendous power in the world that it has since become. We find it difficult to realise that, in its beginnings, the Christian Church was, in comparison with what it has since become, scarcely more than a grain of mustard seed. To the wealthy, cultured Roman, the earliest Christians were but an obscure and ignorant sect of Jewish fanatics only noticeable because of the disturbances they brought about to law and order.

All this we may know, but find it difficult, almost impossible, to realize. Hence our sense of shock, as at the sound of a thunderclap heard in a cloudless sky, when we read the conclusion to the *Procurator of Judea*.

" ' Jesus ? ' " [said Pontius Pilate], " ' Jesus of Nazareth ?   I cannot call him to mind.' "

In other words, the crucifixion of Jesus of Nazareth aroused about as much interest in the cultured Roman of those days, as a brief announcement in a remote corner of *The Times* of the execution of some obscure criminal would excite in our own.

But while his *Histoire Contemporaine* was appearing, and for many years previously, Monsieur France had been steadily accumulating the materials for a great, we may even say a monumental, contribution to the history of his country. Strange, even incongruous as it may appear, the author of *The Rôtisserie de la Reine Pédauque* had long had it in mind to write a Life of Joan of Arc, and with this object in view he had assiduously studied the story of the Maid as revealed by ancient documents; he had visited and impregnated himself with the atmosphere of those regions of France with which she had been associated. His aim was to reconstruct her epoch, to translate himself, so to speak, into the fifteenth century, and to present a veracious history of the age in a spirit of impartiality remote alike from the legends of the hagiographer and the attacks of the iconoclast.

It must be left for more learned critics than I to decide how far Monsieur France has succeeded in the task he has set before himself. What is certain, however, is that he approached that task with a passionate veneration for the subject of it. As long ago as 1886 we find him writing thus in *Le Temps*.

"A mass was celebrated at Notre-Dame des Victories, on Monday 30th May, in commemoration of the four hundred and fifty-fifth anniversary of the death of Joan of Arc. The Church does honour to this saint; our country and humanity at large owe her the most pious homage. She gave

N

us back our land, and displayed to the world what
great things can be wrought by love. I cannot
forbear to dwell with you for a moment upon this
beautiful memory. You are told that there are
two Frances, the Old and the New; that the New
is good and the Old bad. Do not believe it. There
is only one France. It has developed; but it has
not changed its nature. The soul of Old France
was charming. It became incarnate in a shepherd
girl, and then was seen the sweetest, most ingenuous,
the daintiest and most generous being that ever
lived upon this earth. Jeanne, in her day, was the
best creature in France, but everyone throughout
the realm, resembled her. She represented the
mind of all her race; she bore within her the genius
of all. That is why she was obeyed and followed."

These two volumes, richly encrusted as they are
with antiquarian lore, glowing with the shadowy
splendours of those old romantic days, do not, and
could not, contain a finer summing-up of the character and influence of the immortal Maid than
that fugitive and half-forgotten paragraph in *Le
Temps.*

CHAPTER XIII

THE CRITIC

N the *Revue des Deux Mondes* of the 1st of January, 1892, Monsieur Ferdinand Brunetière hurled some rather terrifying thunder at Monsieur Anatole France. To say that Monsieur Brunetière did not approve of Monsieur France's critical methods would be to understate the case. He considered them not only unsound, but immoral. The thunder was loud, the earth trembled, but what lightning there was proved strangely harmless. It merely stimulated Monsieur France to pen a little essay on the functions of criticism, which is at once so witty and so sensible, so humorous and so skilful, so airy and so urbane, that it recalls, in tone and temper, that incomparable example of the controversial manner—Matthew Arnold's reply to the erudite but ponderous Francis Newman.

Monsieur France's little essay, which is prefixed to the third volume of *Life and Letters*, is, in fact, and notwithstanding its light and bantering tone, a very serious contribution to the science and art of criticism. Along with Anatole France, the august

and somewhat Olympian gentleman who sat in the
editorial chair of the *Revue des Deux Mondes* had
included in his indictment the names of two other
offenders : Monsieur Jules Lemaître and Monsieur
Paul Desjardins.   All three had been denounced by
Monsieur Brunetière as guilty of subjective and
personal criticism and as corrupters of youth.   In a
preliminary paragraph, Monsieur France explains
the reasons which led him to dissociate himself from
the alliance of these companions in crime and to face,
unaided and alone, the fulminations of Monsieur
Brunetière.   " Monsieur Lemaître," he says, " is a
modern and a humanist.   He respects tradition and
loves novelty.   He has an open mind, with a taste
for beliefs.   His criticism, indulgent as it is, even
when he is employing irony, is, if correctly assessed,
objective enough.   I cannot quite understand what
it is that annoys Monsieur Brunetière in his manner,
unless it is, perhaps, a certain restless gaiety, as of a
young fawn."

" As for Monsieur Paul Desjardins," he continues,
" with whatever he may be reproached, it certainly
cannot be with too frolicsome a gaiety.   He is
severe, and does not like people to write.   For him,
literature is the Beast of the Apocalypse.   A well-
turned phrase strikes him as a public danger.   He
reminds me of the dismal Tertullian who stated
that the Holy Virgin could not have been beautiful,

otherwise she would have been desired, which is unimaginable. According to Monsieur Paul Desjardins, style is evil. Yet Monsieur Paul Desjardins himself has style, so true it is that the human soul is full of contradictions. His humour being what it is, his advice must not be asked on subjects so frivolous and profane as literature. He does not criticize ; he anathematizes, without hatred. Pale and melancholy, he goes his way scattering compassionate maledictions. By what turn of Fortune's wheel does he find himself burdened with a share of the charges that are heaped upon me, precisely when he declares, in his articles and in his lectures, that I am the barren fig tree of Holy Writ ? With what shuddering horror must he appeal to the man who brackets us, and say to him, *Judica me, et discerne causam meam de gente non sancta ?* "

Whatever Anatole France, in his attitude to literature, may have had in common with Jules Lemaître—and we think that perhaps it was not a little—with Monsieur Desjardins, if it indeed be true that " a well-turned phrase strikes him as a public danger," he certainly had nothing at all. But it is important to consider and, if possible, to define, in what, precisely, this subjective criticism consists which Monsieur France professes and which called for such profound and unqualified disapproval from Monsieur Brunetière. We may get a hint of

it from the following passage from *The Garden of
Epicurus :* " These signs (printed characters) awake
in us divine energies. That is the miracle. A
beautiful verse is like a violin bow drawn across the
resonant fibres of our soul. It is not his own
thoughts, but ours, that the Poet sets singing within
us. When he tells us of a woman he loves, it is our
own loves and griefs he awakens entrancingly in our
souls. He is an evoker of spirits. When we understand him, we are as much poets as he. We have
in us, every one of us, a copy of each of our poets
which no man knows of and which will perish utterly
and for ever with all its variants when we shall cease
to feel and know. And do you suppose we should
love our lyric bards so fondly if they spoke to us of
aught else but our own selves ? " That is a passage
which deserves most careful scrutiny at the hands of
all who would understand France's attitude not only
towards literature but towards life itself. Not only
the thoughts of the Poets, the ideas of the Philosophers, but the very objective and tangible things
of the material world have a separate significance
and a separate message in the mind of each individual beholder. The reader will recall the passage
towards the end of *The Amethyst Ring* when Monsieur Bergeret is about to quit the provincial city
in which he had taught for fifteen years, in order to
take up his new professorial duties at the Sorbonne.

" Come now," said Monsieur Bergeret to himself,
" here is a town in which I have lived for fifteen
years, and which suddenly becomes strange to me
because I am about to leave it. Now that it is no
longer my own town, it ceases to exist, and is
nothing but a vain image. The reason is that the
many interesting things it contains were only
interesting in so far as they directly affected me. . . .
It was peopled by myself alone; I was the only
cause of its existence. It is high time for me to
go; the town is fading away. I never knew that
my mind was subjective to such a mad extent."

   It is small wonder, then, that Anatole France (for
if the voice is the voice of Bergeret the thoughts
are those of his creator), with such ideas as these
about the solid material universe, should have small
sympathy with those who would regard objectively
the airy things of the mind. If the world itself
seems rather than is, if it is but the baseless fabric
of a vision, if, like Clement of Alexandria, we hold
that the objects we contemplate have none but an
ideal existence, what can we say of the things of
the mind but that they are the shadow of a shadow,
the dream of a dream, intimate, personal and incommunicable ?

   If it be true that, as Matthew Arnold de-
fines it, criticism is " a disinterested endeavour to
learn and propagate the best that is known and

thought in the world," how better can we hand on
this knowledge to others than by endeavouring to
make known the effect that such things have had
upon ourselves ? And how many, or rather how few,
are they who turn to books for solace or for inspiration, for aught indeed save idle amusement or
utilitarian instruction ? And these few are not
always, or perhaps even usually, to be found among
the professed exponents of literature; the most
illuminating commentator on the works of the great
masters is Life itself, and the critics are often so
busy with their trade that they have no time to
look round at the world about them. They are so
studious that they keep their study lamp burning
and their shutters closed long after the sun has
risen. They shut out the air, they are deaf to the
stir of the outer world. " When he [the Poet] tells
us of a woman he loves," says Monsieur France in
the passage we have quoted above, " it is our loves
and griefs he awakens so entrancingly in our souls."
Yes, but to know love and grief we must at least
live, and that is what so many of our would-be
guides in literature forget to do. And to live is to
suffer, as Monsieur France knows well, and as he
tells us in an unforgettable passage. " Amidst the
eternal that envelops us," he says, " one thing is
certain—suffering. It is the corner-stone of Life.
On it humanity is founded as on a firm rock.—

Outside it all is uncertainty. It is the sole evidence
of a reality that eludes us. We know that we suffer,
and we know nothing else. This is the base on
which man has built everything. Yes, it is on the
parched granite of pain that man has firmly established love and courage, heroism and pity, the choir
of august laws and the procession of terrible or
delightful virtues. If that foundation failed them,
those noble figues would all crash together into the
abyss of nothingness. Humanity has an obscure
consciousness of the necessity of pain. It has placed
pious sorrow among the virtues of the saints.
Blessed are they that suffer, and woe to the fortunate ! Because it uttered that cry, the Gospel has
reigned over the world for two thousand years."

But the broad question of the relation of literature to life, and France's attitude towards this
question, concerns, rather, his philosophy. To that
we shall return later. In a sense all true literature
is criticism—criticism of life, but for the moment
we are concerned, in a narrower sense, with his
critical method and his critical achievements.

His critical work, in this more restricted sense, is
mainly comprised in the *préfaces* which have been
collected in the volume given to the public under
the title of *The Latin Genius*, and in the four
volumes entitled *Life and Letters*, which are made
up of the weekly causeries he contributed as literary

critic of *Le Temps*. That these papers, written at regular weekly intervals, should hold a place in the forefront of Monsieur France's work, that they still excite an interest as fresh and engaging as the day on which they appeared, is sufficient proof that they are infinitely more than mere readable journalism, and stamps their author as the worthy successor of Sainte-Beuve, that exemplar of critics, whose task, after an interval of twenty years, he was called on to assume.

I believe that the practised reviewer, one who has got his hand well in, thinks little of " reviewing " half a dozen books in a morning ; perhaps more, if they are well provided with indexes. One well-known critic of recent years boasted that, in his journalistic lifetime, he had " noticed " the incredible total of thirty thousand books. Truly, such a calling is no sinecure. If it merely amounted to this, that the book worth writing about came, by some favour of the gods, without delay and without trouble, into one's very hands, then perhaps it would not be an undue tax upon a man to write a *causerie* every seven days on such a book. But, when we remember that, for every book selected, there must be, at a modest computation, ten set aside ; when, moreover, we bear in mind that, if the work is to be done with credit to the reviewer and profit to the reader, the book must not merely be read, but studied, it is evident that the writing of a weekly *chronique des livres* is a task that calls for a considerable measure of patience and skill. It will be of interest, therefore, to learn how Anatole France regarded his task. It happens that, in May 1870, he began a series of articles on " Books of the Month," and this series he prefaced with the following remarks :

" Well-bred people in the seventeenth century had a delightful way of expressing quiet approval of people with whom they liked to have friendly intercourse. It used to be said, in those days, that a man who was acquainted with the usages of good soceity, and took an interest in things of the mind, was an *honnête homme*, an honest man. Racine was a very *honnête homme*, who wrote fine poetry. Thus it was that he went to the Louvre, although he was but of middling birth. To pass for an *honnête homme*, one had to be endowed with a delicate sense of the beautiful, which is the charm of life. Although our generation has turned out *honnêtes gens* at a lower price, we have, thank God, a few possessed of the qualities which Monsieur de la Rochefoucauld or Mlle de Scudéry would have desired in them. The *honnêtes gens* of the seventeenth century, men of leisure, read and wrote long letters on literary novelties ; our *honnêtes gens* (using this title in its old-fashioned acceptation) write fewer letters and read more articles. It seems to me that, to write in a review like the *Bibliophile français*, is to hold converse with them, and that it is they whom one must do one's utmost not to offend.

" We do not think that a review of the books of the month should be anything but a friendly conversation carried on in a tone suitable to the subject, but untrammelled by any system or theory.

" A task of this nature will gain, as we think, in charm and sincerity if we express our ideas and impressions, as they come to us, without any obvious æsthetic restriction. . . .

" It will be our care only to put before our readers such books as we consider worthy their interest.

" Furthermore, we hold that this interest extends over the whole domain of arts and letters. Nowadays, when writers freely take an interest in the plastic arts, and when artists are sometimes very literary, there scarcely remain any boundary lines between the arts, and a literary critic, if he is to do his work well, must visit the museums with almost as much assiduity as he visits libraries. We shall, then, when occasion demands, pass from History to the Fine Arts, and from the Fine Arts to Poetry, and the title *Bibliophile français*, which will appear on each of our pages, will be no tax upon us in our various disquisitions, but will remind us, on the contrary, that every book worthy of the name is open to our predilection or our curiosity."

It may be well, however, to pause for a moment, in order to give a brief account of the nature of this objective criticism of which Monsieur Brunetière thinks so highly but which Monsieur France regards as non-existent.

When the reviewer, the conscientious reviewer, has given us his account of a book; when he has indicated its subject-matter; when he has pointed out the merits or demerits of its style; when he has " placed " the work in relation to other productions of a similar nature, he has performed as much as may reasonably be expected of him. This, essentially, is objective criticism. The critic will say whether the book is to be admired or condemned, and why; basing his conclusions not on any predilections of his own—his personal sympathies or antipathies must, indeed, be rigidly excluded—but on certain criteria traditional with the organ in which he is writing, or with the school of thought of which he is an exponent. He is not encouraged to digress, to indulge in asides, in confidences. The critic is a judge. He is presumed to have proved his right to wear the ermine. His experience and that of his colleagues on the bench have probably taught him to regard most books that are brought before him with suspicion, and in his heart he will be disposed

to " damn them at a venture." Like the young
critic who did not shrink from laying down the law
to Monsieur Sylvestre Bonnard, he will " point out
every error with a remarkably lucid power of
incisive criticism." And just as a judge is strictly
bound by law as to what is admissible or inadmissible
as evidence, so is your objective critic obliged or
expected to deliver his verdict in accordance with
certain time-honoured, traditional and supposedly
immutable tests. His tendencies are prone to be
conservative, even hide-bound, and his pronounce-
ments are not always free from a certain assumption
of omniscience, expressed or implied. Like Omar's
master potter, *he knows*. Not of this school is
Anatole France ; emphatically not of this school.
Criticism he holds, like philosophy and history, to be
" a sort of romance designed for those who have
sagacious and inquiring minds, and every romance is,
rightly taken, an autobiography. The good critic
is he who relates the adventures of his own soul
among masterpieces." The phrase was notable,
but it was followed, hard upon, by one more notable
still. " Objective criticism," he went on to assert,
" has no more existence than objective art, and all
those who deceive themselves into the belief that
they put anything but their own personalities into
their work are dupes of the most fallacious of
illusions." It sounded like rank heresy. It could

not, and did not, fail to arouse the Brunetièrean
indignation. As we have recorded, the thunder
rattled, the lightning flashed, the fire ran along the
ground. When it was all over, the object of these
fulminations stood smiling and unscathed.

And yet Monsieur Brunetière had right on his
side after all. At least he was not wholly wrong.
There *is* such a thing as objective criticism. It has
crippled at birth many a writer who deserved a
better fate; it has given a vogue to many who
merited a far worse one. But on the whole, and
despite these occasional miscarriages of justice,
objective criticism has a being, and it is well that the
majority of reviewers should practise it. It is not
everyone whose " adventures among masterpieces "
we should follow with any great degree of excite-
ment; not everyone to whom we should be prepared to listen with pleasurable anticipation when
he announced that he was going to speak of himself
à propos of Shakespeare, *à propos* of Racine, or of
Pascal or of Goethe, for not every one is, like Anatole
France, both a scholar and a man of the world, a
lover of books and a lover of life. The combina-
tion is exceedingly rare, almost as seemingly impossible as that ideal drink which, according to some
wit, should combine the attributes of making one
drunk and keeping one sober to enjoy it. Monsieur
France never suffers his interest or enthusiasm con-

cerning life to disturb his poise. Though he has somewhere said that the only childish people are those who never act like children, he always knows when he is playing the fool.

What may be called the " cloistered scholar " legend of Anatole France we shall have occasion to refer to at length later on. It is as misleading as it is widespread. " There are bookish souls for whom the universe is but paper and ink," says Monsieur France. But he himself is not of these. " The man whose body is animated by such a soul," he adds, " spends his life before his desk without any care for the realities whose graphic representation he studies so obstinately. Of the beauty of women, he knows only what has been written about it He is monstrous and ignorant. He has never looked out of the window." Monsieur France is right. Truly there is no ignorance so deadly as the ignorance of the learned. When Monsieur France tells us that he will talk of himself *à propos* of this masterpiece or of that, it is rather that he makes a book the occasion of entertaining us with some intimate reflections about life, not his own life only, but the experience common to all the sons of Adam and to all the daughters of Eve. This it is that gives the note of universality to his writings. French, indeed, he is in the structure and movement of his sentences; French in the passionate love of country, the

" amour sacré de la patrie " that animates him;
French in his profound reverence, his " desperate
love " as he calls it, for Latin culture; yet this
Frenchman, who says " the milk of the Roman
Wolf forms part of our blood," who speaks of the
" complexities " and the " confusion " which prevail
in English literature, who refers to the " phantoms
of ideas in *Hamlet* as more impalpable than the
ghost that wanders on the terrace at Elsinore " is
so akin to the English spirit, so *sympathique* to
the hearts of Englishmen, not, assuredly, because
his language is " complex " or " confused," for
never was there a style of more luminous purity, but
because of a profound yet humorous sincerity in his
attitude towards life and—beneath all the classical
elegance of his writings—a certain quality of home-
liness in the expression of it which, in varying
degrees, are characteristic of English literature from
Shakespeare to Dickens.

The charm of Monsieur France's critical method
lies in the absence, or apparent absence, of method.
These contributions to *Le Temps* are, in very truth,
causeries. He talks as easily and as unrestrainedly as
he might chat to some old friend of his college days
after dinner. There is no constraint in the atmosphere, nothing didactic, nothing professorial. Like
Charles Lamb, he is not above stooping " to catch a
glittering something in your presence, to share it

with you, before he quite knows whether it be true touch or not." Perfectly at our ease, we may settle ourselves down in our armchair with a feeling of complete confidence in the performance and the performer. It will be informal, but the touch will be sure. We know from experience that there will never be a harsh or a jarring note. Amused tolerance, balanced judgment, mellow wisdom, effortless phrasing, learning profound but unobtrusive, and last but perhaps most important of all, rich and exquisite humour. Such, set down in cold enumeration, are the qualities with which he illumines the subject of Life and Letters; such are the qualities, but how delicately, how miraculously blended! If the wisdom had been grimmer, the learning more ponderous, the humour less unforced, the effect would have been marred. We should have felt that he was addressing not a friend, not ourselves, but an audience. Monsieur France never mounts the rostrum. He never seems so remote but that he could, if he had a mind, lean over and lay a friendly hand upon our knee. He never has to raise his voice, to declaim. He is a friend, not a lecturer. He does not inculcate lessons or enunciate theories. His conversation is gracious, persuasive, modest. You need not fear, when you enter into his presence, that the atmosphere is going to be frigidly intellectual or of that comfortless

quality which the Americans call "highbrow."
Nevertheless, because these little essays are utterly
natural and unforced, it must not be supposed that
there is no art in them. On the contrary, there is a
very great deal. But so perfect is it that it is not
discernible. Yet even this requires correction.
When we say there is art in these *causeries* we do
not mean in the plan, in the structure of them.
They flow on with the unpremeditated ease of
familiar conversation. The art is in the language,
in the style. The structure is, apparently, the most
artless thing in the world. For example a "notice"
of a modern novel—*Mensonges* by Paul Bourget,
a story of passion, jealousy and disillusionment—
becomes a meditation on à Kempis's *Imitation.*
"Is it not wonderful," he observes, "that the
Imitation, written in an age of faith by a humble
ascetic for pious and solitary souls, should be admirably suited to-day to sceptics and people of the
world. A pure deist or peaceful atheist can make
it his bedside book. . . . The lonely monk, whose
work it is, . . . knew life profoundly. He had
penetrated to the secrets of the soul and of the
senses. Nothing in the world of appearances,
amid which we struggle with cruel weakness and
touching illusions was hidden from him. . . . His
book is the book of the best of men, since it is the
book of the unhappy. There is no surer counsellor

and no more intimate consoler. Ah, if Monsieur Paul Bourget's hero . . . had read over every morning the eighth chapter of the *Imitation,* if he had sought his joy in sadness and his pleasure in renunciation, he would not have tasted the worst of all sorrows, the only sorrow which is truly evil, the sorrow which does not purify but defiles, and he would not have endeavoured to die the death of the despairing." This is a typical example of Monsieur France's manner. It is the manner of one for whom great literature is not merely a pastime, an adornment, but a reality, a religion. In this little essay, there are not more than six pages of it, we learn much about Monsieur Bourget's book, which is well; but we learn more about Anatole France, which is better. We learn, for example, how it is he comes to be described as a pagan " haunted by the preoccupation of Christ."

A book is valuable in proportion to the emotions it stirs, to the associations it quickens in the mind of him who reads it. " When you read a book," says Anatole France, " you read it how you please, you read in it, or rather into it, what you choose." There is no rigid, immutable, external standard by which a book may be judged. Even the *securus judicat orbis terrarum* of Saint Augustine will not avail, nor is there, as Matthew Arnold would have it there was, any sort of collective, intellectual tribunal from which there is no appeal. " What," asks Monsieur France, " is a book ? A series of little printed signs— essentially only that. It is for the reader to supply himself the forms and colours and sentiments to which these signs correspond. It will depend on him whether the book be dull or brilliant, hot with passion or cold as ice. Or, if you would prefer to put it otherwise, each word in a book is a magic finger that sets a fibre of our brain vibrating like a harp string, and so evokes a note from the sounding-board of our own soul. No matter how skilful, how inspired the artist's hand, the sound it awakes depends on the quality of the strings within our-selves." The truth is, perhaps, rather that litera-ture and life react perpetually one upon the other, mutually enriching and illuminating each other. The world is richer, more full of significance for the lettered than the unlettered man, and, on the other hand, it is no less true that books withhold their profounder beauty, their more intimate secrets, from him who knows not Life.

Literature has been described as that which sundry men and women have written memorably about Life, and we need seek no better definition. This then is the critic's function : to interpret books in the light of life, of life as he knows it and has experienced it. In the case of Anatole France knowledge of literature and knowledge of life have united and taken root in a singularly gifted mind, and from their union has been born a series of meditations on Life and Letters, so wise, so gracious, so informing and, withal, so friendly and so human, that, for all their seemingly ephemeral character, they are likely to endure long after works more expressly designed for immortality have sunk into oblivion.

CHAPTER XIV

THE PHILOSOPHER

THE nineteenth century produced two writers of genius—one an Englishman and the other a Frenchman—who, though in many respects as wide as the poles asunder, nevertheless present some conspicuous points of resemblance. Both are steeped in Græco-Latin culture; both, in their respective languages, are the greatest prose writers of their era; both hold identical views concerning the principles of literary art, and both achieve consummate ease and grace of style by taking infinite pains with their work. Nor does the likeness end here. For while both possess commanding intellects, both set the dictates of heart above the conclusions of reason and, if one may be called the most Christian of sceptics, the other was perhaps the most sceptical of Christians. Of these men, one— John Henry Newman—became a Prince, and the other—Anatole France—an outlaw, of the Church; yet the motto chosen by the former for his Cardinal's shield *Cor ad cor loquitur*—Heart speaketh to Heart,

might be adopted with hardly less fitness by the latter. But while Newman's whole life, all his energies, all his culture, all his genius were centred on showing forth what he held to be the divine character and triumphant destiny of the Roman Church, France, though perhaps he caught a glimpse of the vision, put it early by and has remained ever since a spectator, an amused and tolerant, an indolent and gently ironic spectator, of the tragi-comedy of life, smiling indulgently, and a little sadly, alike at the enthusiasms and the weaknesses of his fellowmen, holding steadfastly to but one conviction—that man and his most enduring monuments are but as the reed shaken by the wind and doomed to wither as the flowers of the field. Well it was that he chose as the keynote of his *Garden of Epicurus*—the book in which he records —not indeed his philosophy, for he had none—but his reflections about life—this passage from *La Lampe d'Argile* by Frédéric Plessis : " Why have we not known your dainty caresses, O scented airs of the ancient garden, O breezes of Cecrops, divine harbingers; ye who tempted in olden days the Latin bard ! 'Tis thence our eyes, in a tranquil smile, might have beheld afar off the errors of mortal men,—ambition and love, well matched in their frenzy, and the unavailing incense burned on the altars."

Anatole France is, indeed, much more a poet than a philosopher. Profoundly impressed as he is with the impermanence, the ceaseless and ineluctable mutability of the things of this world, he believes in making the most of the fleeting hour. And, being a poet, he is a man of complex and ever-changing moods, shunning the absolute alike in affirmation and in negation. He is full of reservations, of qualifications, and what he advances on this page, he will half retract on the next. His mind has been well compared by a French critic to a pair of scales so delicately balanced that they seem as though they would never cease their oscillations.

But the philosophers and their systems Anatole France holds in small esteem. " Philosophical systems," he says, " are interesting only as psychical documents, well adapted to enlighten the savant on the different conditions which the human mind has passed through. Valuable for the study of man, they afford us no information about anything that is not man." Of metaphysicians he has no better opinion : " The very metaphysicians " he says, " who think to escape the world of appearances, are constrained to think in allegory. A sorry sort of poets, they dim the colours of the ancient fables and are themselves but gatherers of fables. Their output is mythology without body or blood."

And Science, what has that done for man, but illumine the darkness that enshrouds him, and enable him to discern a few fixed relationships in the infinite complexity of the phenomena by which he is encompassed?

"We are done now," he cries, "with the twelve spheres and the planets under which man were born happy or unhappy, jovial or saturnine. The solid vault of the firmament is cleft asunder. Our eyes and thoughts plunge into the infinite abysses of the heavens. Beyond the planets, we discover, instead of the Empyrean of the elect and the angels, a hundred millions of suns rolling through space, escorted, each, by its own procession of dim satellites invisible to us. Amidst this infinity of systems, *our* Sun is but a bubble of gas and the Earth a drop of mud." Such considerations as these, and the consciousness of the incessant changes taking place in all about him, the frailty of human life, the evanescence of beautiful things, form the ever-recurring burden of his writings. "Verweile doch Du bist so schön" we seem to hear him cry from a heart full of love and longing. There is nothing, nothing that will endure. "There was a time when our planet was not suitable for mankind; it was too hot and too moist. A time will come when it will cease to be suitable; it will be too cold and dry. When the sun goes out—a catastrophe that is

bound to be—mankind will have long ago disappeared. The last inhabitants of the earth will be
as destitute and as ignorant, as feeble and dull-
witted as the first. They will have forgotten all
the arts and all the sciences. They will huddle
wretchedly in caves alongside the glaciers that will
then roll their transparent masses over the half-
obliterated ruins of the cities where now men think
and love, suffer and hope. . . . The last desperate
survivors of human kind—desperate without so
much as realizing why or wherefore—will know
nothing of us, nothing of our genius, nothing of our
love. . . . One day the last survivor, callous alike
to hate and love, will exhale to the unfriendly sky
the last human breath. And the globe will go
rolling on, bearing with it through the silent fields
of space, the ashes of humanity, the poems of Homer
and the august remnants of the Greek marbles,
frozen to its icy surfaces. No thought will ever
again rise towards the infinite from the bosom of the
dead world, where the soul has dared so much. . . ."

Not, it must be confessed, an exhilarating subject
for meditation. Fortunately for the human race,
the doom which is here pronounced in language
of such harmonious solemnity is not yet imminent.
Monsieur France wisely refuses to suffer his spirits
to be too greatly oppressed by these lugubrious
considerations. The thought that all things come

to an end sooner or later, and sooner still the individual's capacity to enjoy them, does but render them the dearer in his sight, and cheerfully he sets himself " to love that well, which he must leave ere long." " We shall all be swallowed up one day," he says, " every one of us, and we know it : the wisest thing is to forget about it." And so he surrounds himself with all manner of things good to look upon. Books in rich bindings, magnificent folios, rare *incunabula*, carvings, statues, pictures, mediæval furniture, tapestry and all kinds of beautiful or curious memorials of the past. It is a taste he acquired early and it has grown on him. He is an inveterate collector.

A French writer of the younger school, Monsieur Henri Massis, has recently had some rather severe things to say about Monsieur Anatole France, and he has said them with that earnestness and austere ardour which are so often the accompaniments of youth. When the young are serious they are very serious indeed. This is the case with Monsieur Massis. He complains that Monsieur France is a pessimist and that all his writings issue in sterility, lose themselves in nescience. Monsieur Massis indeed concedes that for more than thirty years the name of Anatole France has stood in the estimation of the world for all that is most exquisite and most refined in the French language ; he confesses

ANATOLE FRANCE'S WRITING DESK

By the kind permission of " The Paris and London Studio."

that Anatole France has exerted over the minds
of his own and succeeding generations an intellectual
influence second to none, and that he has enjoyed
a prestige comparable only to that of Voltaire; but
in spite of all this, which, to say the least, strikes
us as no mean achievement, Monsieur Massis
remains unsatisfied. He has, we repeat, weighed
Monsieur France in the balance and found him
lamentably wanting. He quotes with apparent
approval, the opinions expressed by several prominent writers " who were in their twenties about
1885 and who then gave utterance to their gratitude
to Monsieur France because he had rescued them
from the abjectness and poverty of the prevailing
school and, in place of the ' literature of the illiterate,"
had once more restored to its place in men's hearts
the sovereign genius of the language and art of
France." But this, it seems, is not enough. The
youth of France cried out for bread and the author
of *Thaïs* has given them, not indeed stones, but
pictures, for all the world as though they were
children to be kept amused. Monsieur France,
and this is the head and front of his offending, has
neither embraced an old philosophy nor formulated
a new one. He has, save indeed on one or two rare
but important occasions, refrained from taking
sides in any of the great issues that have agitated
his fellow-citizens, and when he has espoused a

cause it has usually been an unpopular one—*sed victa Catoni*. Consequently he has incurred the displeasure of many priests and partisans. He has dared to be independent in the land of Liberty; to combat injustice in the land of Equality; to show compassion in the land of Fraternity. Naturally the official champions of these excellent virtues view him with a hostile eye. Monsieur Massis, at any rate, displays impatience with Monsieur France because he is not moved by those passionate ideals which stir men to missions or to martyrdom. It is true that Monsieur France has pointed out that a man who is so sure of his own opinions as to be ready to die for them is not free from a certain trace of self-conceit and that, on the whole, saints are not very easy people to get on with, not " clubable " as one might say; but, even so, the reproof seems scarcely just. It seems to forget, or to ignore, the fact that when a sentence of monumental injustice clamoured for reversal, it was this cultured voluptuary, this dilettante, this indolent hedonist who entered the fray and fought with energy and effect against the embattled hosts of tyranny, bigotry and falsehood.

Nevertheless, it is true that Monsieur France brings us no constructive philosophy, no system, no creed, no unfaltering answer to the riddle of life. In a sentence which is almost a literal translation of

a famous quatrain of Omar Khayam he says : " I
have asked my way of all, priests, savants, magicians
or philosophers, who claim to know the geography
of the Unknown.   None of them has been able
to give me any definite indication of the right road."
It was not always so.   When certain solemn gentle-
men who were examining him for his *Baccalauréat* asked him to demonstrate the existence
of God, he did so out of hand.   But those were the
days when he doggedly declined to employ the note
of interrogation in his exercises.   His mother looking
over one of his efforts, rebuked him for leaving out
the note of interrogation after the sentence " What
is God ? "   " My answer," says Monsieur France,
" was noble : ' I am not asking,' I said proudly,
' I know.' "

" I have changed a great deal since then," he
adds.   " I never refuse, now, to put notes of
interrogation in the places where it is customary
to employ them.   I am sorely tempted, indeed,
to add very big ones after everything I write, or say,
or think.   Perhaps, if she were alive to-day, my
dear mother would say that I use too many."
" I have," he says, " turned my eyes more than once
in the direction of absolute scepticism, but I never
entered there.   I was afraid of losing my foothold
on that foundation which swallows up everything
that is placed upon it.   I have been afraid of those

two words that are so terrible in their sterility—
' I doubt.' So mighty are they that the mouth
which has once pronounced them clearly, is sealed
for ever and can never break silence again. If
we doubt, we must perforce keep silent, for whatever
the nature of our discourse, to speak is to affirm.
And since I lacked courage for silence and renounce-
ment, I had made up my mind to believe and I
believed. At all events I believed in the relativity
of things and in the succession of phenomena."

The words which Pascal employed concerning
Montaigne might be used with equal justice of
Anatole France : " He involves all things in such
universal, unmingled scepticism as to doubt of his
very doubts." It is true that Anatole France is
so complete a sceptic that he sometimes seems
inclined to question his own unbelief :

> . . . a sunset touch,
> A fancy from a flower-bell, someone's death,
> A chorus-ending from Euripides,

such things as these seem to bring the eternal note
of interrogation into his mind again, " just when
he's safest." In the scepticism of Anatole France
there is nothing hard or rigid, or pedantic or self-
sufficient. Despite his attacks upon the Church—
and in some of them his taste seems to have stumbled
a little—he seems, as someone has well said, to be
" haunted by the preoccupation of Christ," *anima*

naturaliter Christiana. How else could he have written this :

" Suffering, Pain—how divine it is, how misunderstood ! To it we owe all that is good in us, all that makes life worth living; to it we owe pity, and courage, and all the virtues. The earth is but a grain of sand in the barren infinity of worlds. Yet if it is only on the earth that creatures suffer, it is greater than all the rest of the universe put together."

Or again this, of Pity :

" It is through pity we remain truly men. Let us not change into stone like the defiers of the gods in the old myths. Let us commiserate the weak because they suffer persecution, and the fortunate of this world because it is written : ' Woe unto you that laugh.' Let us choose the good part, which is to suffer with them that suffer, and let us say with lips and heart to the victims of calamity, like the good Christian to Mary, ' *Fac me tecum plangere,*'—Make me to lament with thee."

Somewhat too much has been made of what is called Monsieur France's " Nihilism." We are told, for example, how, with his " universal raillery," he saps the base of every institution, the foundation of every belief. He is represented as a sort of knight-errant riding over the world, ever on the look-out for something to tilt at. No tradition so august, no

P

opinion so well established, but he will couch the lance
of his mockery against it and bring it ignominiously
to the ground. But it is not merely your beliefs
or mine that he treats thus, but also, and primarily,
his own. He is for ever saying to himself, when an
idea catches his fancy, " Nay, not so fast, my friend ;
there is another side to the question. Let us give
due weight to it." The fact is that Monsieur
France is too susceptible of ideas, and looks out
with too comprehensive an eye over the field of
human endeavour to hold any opinion with ardour
or to hold it long. " As for myself," says Jérôme
Coignard to Mr. Rockstrong, " I feel that my
intelligence is quite spoilt by reflection. And as it
is not in the nature of mankind to think with any
profundity, I own that my leaning to thought is an
odd mania and highly inconvenient. In the first
place," he continues, " it makes me unfit for any
undertaking, for our actions result from a limited
outlook and a narrow way of thinking. . . .
Reflection would hamper me from the outset, and
I should find reasons for coming to a stop at every
move I made."

" Conscience," says Hamlet, meaning by conscience
what we call consciousness, " makes cowards of us
all, and the native hue of resolution is sicklied o'er
with the pale cast of thought." But with Anatole
France there is no morbid brainsickness, no railing

against Fate. The world is out of joint, true.
But it always was, and probably always will be.
He decides to make the best of it and to laugh at
it and to pity it. " I have no illusions about
mankind, and, so as not to hate them, I despise
them. I despise and pity them. Mutual contempt
means peace on earth, and if men would only
thoroughly despise one another they would do themselves no further harm and live together in an
amiable tranquillity."

It was not merely his schoolmasters at the College
Stanislas that were his " Molières." He has found
plenty of them in the world at large. If his laughter
has at times a hint of sadness in it, it is none the
worse for that. To Anatole France—who has so
keen a sense of proportion, and that is to say of
humour—even the most heroic of us do but strut
and fret our hour upon the stage. It is only the
simple, the lowly, who have a chance of attaining
the sublime. Of all the saints in the calendar, he
loves Saint Francis best, because he was kind to
animals and to the poor. As for knowledge,
philosophy, science, what do the scientists know
with their calculations and fine apparatus for
weighing, seeing, measuring ? " They discover new
relations merely, and are but the plaything of new
illusions." " If I were not convinced, my son," says
the Abbé Coignard to Jacques Tournebroche, " of

the holy truths of our religion, there would be nothing left for me, holding as I do the conviction that all human knowledge is but a progress in phantasmagoria, but to throw myself from this parapet into the Seine, which has seen many others drown since she began to flow, or to go and ask of Catherine that form of oblivion from the ills of this world which one finds in her arms, and for which it would be indecent for me to look, in my position and above all, at my age." Monsieur France, unlike the Abbé, has had no religious truths to fortify him; and if he was called upon to choose between self-annihilation or the pleasures of the senses to bring him solace on this darkling plain swept with confused alarms of struggle and flight, we may be sure that he never for a moment thought of seeking it in the waters of the Seine.

If it be not given to Anatole France to pronounce with the confidence and conviction of the professed believer on the mysteries of Life and Death, and to withdraw the veil that overhangs the destiny of the human soul, he is at least a devoted lover of the Muses.

> Fortunatus et ille deos qui novit agrestes,
> Panaque Silvanumque senem Nymphasque sorores.

If he professes no philosophy, no creed, it is because he has tried them all and discovered none that will unravel the master-knot of human fate. But wherefore complain ?   The fact is that in the course of this journey we call Life, this pilgrimage, the *whence* and *whither* of which are enveloped in obscurity, we shall find him a highly agreeable companion.   He is never dictatorial and never in a hurry.   He is in fact much given to loitering, and if a by-way tempts him, he will readily leave the high-road to explore it.   He will tell many a diverting story of saint and sinner and many of folk who were neither the one nor the other, but a blend of both, like the majority of us.   His polished, urbane discourse, rich with the spoils of Time, though always diverting and profitable, is not invariably what pious folk call " edifying."   In that respect he resembles Shakespeare, Rabelais and Sterne. He is prodigiously learned, but he will never bore you with a display of erudition.   He has indeed rather a contempt for the knowledge-mongers, and we may say of him that he, like Wordsworth :

> " . . . both Man and Boy
> Hath been an idler in the land ;
> Contented if he might enjoy
> The things which others understand."

He is too great to be clever, too wise to be dogmatic.   He is indulgent to all men save the fanatics.   Fanatics he detests because they are the sworn enemies of Beauty, and in his eyes the only unpardonable sins are the sins against Beauty.

" For my part," he says, " if I were called upon to choose between beauty and truth, I should not hesitate; I should hold to beauty, being confident that it bears within it a truth both higher and deeper than truth itself. I will go so far as to say that there is nothing true in the world save beauty."

CHAPTER XV

THE STYLIST

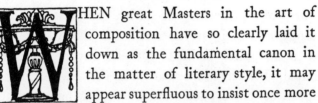HEN great Masters in the art of composition have so clearly laid it down as the fundamental canon in the matter of literary style, it may appear superfluous to insist once more on the indissolubility of the idea from the mode of its expression, of *la forme et le fond* as the French say. We know, or we should know, that, where literary art reaches its most perfect expression, they are inextricably interwoven. Alter so much as a single word, nay, so much as a single vowel sound, and the magic of the passage—supposing it to be of the perfection we have postulated—is marred or destroyed. Like a bird stricken in its flight, its wings droop and it falls lamentably earthwards. For words may be so arranged, by a master's hand, as to give them, beyond their direct and immediate significance, a subtle and illimitable power of suggestion. And this suggestiveness it is, this richness in overtones, to borrow a term from the science of music, which imparts to the work of the

215

great masters, in prose no less than in poetry, its permanence, its abiding charm, its power. This view of the rôle of words, which is at the foundation of the symbolist movement, involves the corollary that the more closely a writer's work approaches perfection, the less is it susceptible of translation. If, by combining, in subtle vowel cadences, the words of a given language, with their history, their traditions, their associations with this writer and with that, their intimate complex flavour, all those impalpable accretions that make them savour, so to speak, of the very soil from which they have sprung, if, by so doing, a writer has succeeded in conveying to those who read his idiom some sense of the idea by which he is animated, of the vision by which he is inspired, how little is it likely that the words of another language, with their different sounds, their different history, their different associations will, even in the hands of the most skilful and sympathetic renderer, afford any but a shadowy and imperfect reflection of the original.

In dealing then with imaginative literature, we must rid ourselves of the notion that there is any such thing as a basic idea independent of and separable from the particular words in which it is clothed and susceptible of being presented with equal power and equal charm—or rather with identical power and identical charm, in other words.

Though this is true of prose no less than of poetry, it is easier perhaps to exemplify from the latter. It does not, for instance, require so very sensitive an ear to detect in the lines which I have seen misquoted thus :

> The moving waters at their priestlike task
> Of *calm* ablution round earth's human shores

a declension from that beauty which is resident in the words which Keats actually wrote :

> The moving waters at their priestlike task
> Of *pure* ablution round earth's human shores.

And in this passage, in which the misquotation—or misprint—also affects only a single syllable, a single vowel sound, the change, the loss, is no less evident—

> Breaking the silence of the seas
> Among the *fur*thest Hebrides

Wordsworth wrote "*far*thest Hebrides." In the present Lord Tennyson's life of his father, the word appears as "furthest," and lo, how the seas are narrowed by that closed vowel sound, and how the magic has died from off the waters and faded into the common light of day! If some there be who hold that it is "to consider too curiously to consider thus," that language is a practical thing intended for practical ends, and that life is too short for such vain and useless refinements, then let them not essay to understand the style of Anatole France, for, we assure them, such things are not

disdained by him. Hear, for example, what he says
of the following lines of La Fontaine—

> .... O belles, évitez
> Le fond des bois et leur vaste silence.

" The epithet *vaste* applied to silence makes it
solemn. Herein lies the whole beauty of this line,
which echoes the *per vasta silentia* of Lucan. Put
profond in place of *vaste*, and the line is hopelessly
spoilt. An analogous example, from Racine, will
help to make this plain. Phèdre has taken poison :
she says, as she expires :

> " Le fer auroit déjà tranché ma destinée
> Mais je laissois gémir la vertu soupçonnée.
> J'ay voulu, devant vous exposant mes remords,
> Par un chemin plus *lent* descendre chez les morts."

The last line has obvious beauty ; we have but to
change two letters to make it mediocre ; put—

> " Par un chemin plus *long* descendre chez les morts,"

and the charm is vanished. The whole charm
came from the word *lent* (slow), which gave the
path of the dead a kind of mysterious life, indefinable, profound. Great beauty in poetry (and
we may add in prose) may be at the same time
beauty of the most delicate." Thus writes Anatole
France, and it is in this spirit that one should
approach the study of his style, for it is a work of
art wrought with the most consummate finish, and
it demands of the reader, if he would enjoy it to

the full, that he should bring to the study of it an insight, a sympathy, a sustained attention commensurate with the care that brought it into being.

Now what strikes an Englishman, generally, in reading the work of French writers, is the uniformly high standard it achieves. It has somewhere been said that it is a difficult thing for a Frenchman to write badly, and it is unquestionably true that the French language does lend itself to a sort of trimness in writing, a sort of neat and balanced clarity, qualities which are rarely absent even from those *roman-feuilletons* whose English counter-parts are usually distinguished by every variety of crudeness and vulgarity. But in spite, or perhaps by reason of, this set standard after which every educated Frenchman is taught by laborious and repeated exercise to strive, the prose of so many French writers, notwithstanding the skill and artistry with which it is composed, exhibits a frigidity, a lack of individuality, as though the author had not so much an idea of his own to unfold as a certain model to which it was his duty, at all costs, to conform. It tends, in a word, to become conventional, almost mechanical, and to lack the personal note; much in the same way as a piece of furniture turned out in a factory, however serviceable and even elegant it may be, lacks the individuality that marks the article patiently fash-

ioned by the craftsman's own hand. " The many,"
says Newman, " use language as they find it; the
man of genius uses it indeed, but subjects it withal
to his own purposes, and moulds it according to his
own peculiarities . . . his views of external things,
his judgments upon life, manners and history, the
exercises of his wit, of his humour, of his depth,
of his sagacity, all these innumerable and incessant
creations, the very pulsation and throbbing of his
intellect, does he image forth, to all does he give
utterance, in a corresponding language which is . . .
the faithful expression of his intense personality,
attending on his own inward world of thought as
its very shadow; so that we might as well say that
one man's shadow is another's as that the style of
a really gifted mind can belong to any but himself.
It follows him about as a shadow. His thought and
feeling are personal and so is his language personal."
Now of all French writers who had attained celebrity
during the last half-century, there is none whose
style is more personal than that of Anatole France.
Of him, if of any man, it may indeed be said that
his style is his shadow, and so true is it that one
seems, as one reads, to be sitting face to face with
him listening to the leisurely modulations of his
musical voice, and conscious of the half-ironical,
half-indulgent gaze of his strangely expressive eyes.
And yet because, with utter singleness of aim, he

strives only to express the vision or the thoughts that are in his mind; because he disdains all extraneous ornament, his language is, in Mathew Arnold's phrase, " of the centre " : it moves with the grace and dignity, with the ease and freedom, that are the distinguishing characteristics of that perfection of intellectual breeding, which, being sure of itself, is free alike from uneasiness or pomposity, and never strains after effect.

The true stylist is delicately alive to the colour and the flavour of every word he uses; he knows the lineage of each, and the traditions that cluster about it. He knows that, in reality, there is no such thing as a synonym; that no word exactly replaces another : he is sensitive to the distinctions, the delicate shades of meaning that mark off one word from another; he is alive to the associations which certain words and turns of phrase will excite in the mind of the cultured reader. He is fastidious without being precious; he is direct without being bald; his watchword is the *simplex munditiis* of the Roman poet. Such are the characteristics which Anatole France admired in a writer, and of which he himself is a shining exponent.

Whence did Anatole France derive his style is a question that has often been asked. Is it original, innate, or is it imitative, and, if the latter, who are his models ?

There are some, diligent tracers of origins, who would track down, with a chill Teutonic pertinacity, the source whence Anatole France obtained not only his style but his ideas. They would—the pastime seems rather a fashionable one just now—make him out something of an imitator and a plagiarist. As for his ideas, and whence they came, what suggested, what prompted them, that has already been touched on in the course of this survey of his work. But once again, there is nothing new under the sun, and if Anatole France sought his subjects in some old legend or Italian tale, it is certain he

> " changed 'em
> or else new form'd 'em "

and is as little, or as much, of a plagiarist as Shakespeare himself. But of his style, which is our immediate concern, what of that? " Ça, c'est du Fénelon ! " says one. " Ça, c'est du Bossuet ! " says another. " Ça, c'est du Renan, du Voltaire," and so on, not even forgetting Zola. Well, I suppose we are all imitators to a certain extent. Newman, for example, took Cicero for his model; yet he is still Newman; Stevenson had many masters, he confesses to playing the sedulous ape. Anatole France may have had as many or more, but he is still, and pre-eminently, Anatole France. Style—true style, as distinguished from *a* style, *a*

THE MASTER IN HIS GARDEN AT LA BÉCHELLERIE

manner—may not be arrived at by a mere mixing
of ingredients. No culinary process will avail
here. It is vain to say " take of this writer so much
and so much of that, and, again, a *quantum suff.* of
that other." Yet this tracing of influences is not
wholly unprofitable, for it is proved that, had
Anatole France never read a line of Homer or Virgil,
or Theocritus; if he had been unacquainted with
Montaigne and Rabelais, Fénelon and Bossuet, for
example, he would never have written like the
Anatole France we know, but it is at least as true
to say that, having read and pondered those authors,
he would never have written as he did had he not
been—Anatole France. If there never was, as
some would have us believe, a writer more derivative,
there never was a writer more original.

Mr. Edmund Gosse has somewhere said that of
all recent French writers of high rank, Monsieur
Anatole France seems to him most like an
Englishman. But need he have added, as he
did, that he doubted whether Monsieur France
would be pleased at the statement? Surely a
country that has produced a Thomas Browne, a
Dryden, a Swift, an Addison, a Sterne, a De
Quincey, a Newman and a Pater, has no need to
be ashamed of its *prosateurs*. Nevertheless it is
currently held, at least in France, that the *art* of
prose composition not only reaches its highest

development in France, but does not so much as exist outside of it. " Il est certain," says a contemporary French critic of high repute " que l'art de la prose tel que l'entendait Flaubert, un art de la prose attentif à des lois musicales aussi rigoureuses que celles des vers, n'existe dans aucun pays de langue slave ou germanique." And elsewhere this same critic refers to " cet art de la prose que les Français sont seuls à pratiquer." This we think is to claim too much for France, or rather to vouchsafe too little to England. We too have our prose writers, who are just as scrupulously fastidious in their choice of words and phrases, who are just as delicately observant of those *lois musicales*, as any French writer could be. But this is a digression.

Interesting then, and diverting as is this search after the models on whom a writer has formed his style, it leaves the great secret still unsolved. That secret dwells inviolate and inviolable within the writer's personality. The qualities which lend charm and power and permanence to great literature are too elusive, too subtle and, at the same time, too simple and too elemental to be analysed or defined.

One is reminded of a story told, I think, of Sir Joshua Reynolds, who was asked to give his opinion of a picture painted by some talented young lady. This young lady was a patient and conscientious student, and she had produced a picture which had been executed with the most praiseworthy exactitude and attention to detail. " Excellent, excellent ! " said the old man, wishing to encourage. " But," he went on doubtfully, " it wants something; it wants, let me see, it wants—why, damn it, madam, it wants *that !* " What *that* was Sir Joshua could not put into words; but he knew; and every artist, be he painter, musician, sculptor or writer, knows what *that* is. The truth is that, in the last resort, a sensitiveness to the finer qualities of literature is innate and incommunicable, and that is the end of the whole matter. No amount of explanation, no wealth of comment will avail. The Golden Bough may not be severed by the axe of exegesis. We can admire, appreciate, savour the style of an Anatole France or a Charles Lamb, we cannot explain it or account for it.

In literature—in life the rule is not of universal application—but, in literature, it may be said that lovers of the same thing are lovers of one another. Particularly is this true of those who have been nourished on the classics, who were taught and who learned with varying degrees of success to understand and to love the great literary masterpieces of Greek and Roman antiquity. Anatole France, for example, is steeped in Virgil. Virgil dwells within him, not shut off in a special compartment in his brain, not kept there, so to speak, " for

Q

reference," but transforming and infusing all his thoughts, tincturing his ideas, modifying his whole attitude towards life. In the half-indulgent, half-wistful compassion with which he looks out over the world, with its high projects coming to naught, its struggles, its futilities, its pathetic failures and its still more pathetic triumphs, its meanness and its greatness, we discern the shadowy countenance of the *anima cortese Mantovana*, "majestic in his sadness at the doubtful doom of human kind." "Even in my schoolboy days," he says, "I conceived an affection for the poets, an affection which happily I have ever since retained. As a boy of seventeen I adored Virgil and I understood him almost as well as if my masters had never expounded him to me." So long as we continue to study the humanities, so long will writers like Anatole France continue to exert over our minds their subtle and indefinable charm.

As if, however, to give the lie to the proposition that the stylist is born, not made, Anatole France has himself laid down some rules for the guidance of those who would practise the art of writing. To begin with, and rather strangely, he would invert the order customarily assigned to genius and talent. "The pride of the romantics," he says, "and the species of literary mysticism which has been the vogue since Chateaubriand, have invested the word

' genius ' with peculiar and mysterious significance.
One might almost regard genius as a sort of exceptional gift bestowed on certain privileged beings
whom we might term super-men." But he has no
more liking for the raw, untutored genius than some
of us have for that rather trying person known as
" nature's gentleman." By talent, however, he
means much more than is usually implied in that
word, he means genius, but genius trained, chiselled,
refined; genius kept within certain reasoned and
self-imposed limits, genius which has ceaselessly
laboured at self-perfection, which has acquired
that indefinable and imponderable quality, that
all-important trifle, namely *taste*. But it must not
be supposed that the conscious care with which he
composed, the almost infinite pains he took with
his writing, had as its result anything save utter
naturalness, perfect simplicity. Anatole France
achieves the crowning triumph of art, its own con-
cealment. That consummate ease and simplicity
which mark his writings are not produced *currente
calamo*. Like Newman, whom, in the perfection
of literary art, if in no other respect, he closely
resembles, he composed with difficulty, often cor-
recting, erasing, interlining till little of the original
manuscript remained. To Anatole France we may
apply Newman's definition of a great author and
say that he " has with him the charm of an incom-

municable simplicity." As for Renan, of whom he might have said, as Dante said of Virgil, " Thou art my master, thou art he who taught me the good style that did me honour," it is the simplicity of his style that excites his admiration. " It is impossible," he says, " to find words of adequate simplicity in which to do honour to the art of Renan, which is the very perfection of simplicity. He mistrusted eloquence and held rhetoric in detestation. His fluid diction is less in the style of the Latins than in that of the Greeks; he always avoided emphasis and declamation. He has put art into all his books, since in all of them he has put order, and has always adapted his style of writing to the subject and always subordinated the parts to the whole. But the work in which his art manifests itself with its greatest charm, that work which all may read and which the cultured prize so dearly, is the *Souvenirs d'Enfance*, those memories of childhood which shine amid his works like the golden flowers amid the rocks of his own Brittany. Of all his books it is the most lovable because, in it, he has put most of himself."

If Monsieur France disdains the impetuous and unpremeditated improvisations of genius and sets above them the chiselled and polished phrase, if in a word, he is a classic rather than a romantic, it is natural and, indeed, inevitable that he should manifest a great reverence for form. Thus as far back as 1867 we find him declaring that " Form is the golden Vase wherein Thought, that fleeting essence, is preserved to Posterity." Thought and the language which clothes it are, he is never weary of insisting, inseparably interwoven. " It were as witless," he exclaims, " to separate words from matter as a perfume from the vial that contains it." And later on he says, " a poem is only beautiful when it possesses beauty of form, since the form of a work of art results from the substance of it and is but the outward expression of the inmost structure; " and again, still later, he cries, " Woe betide him who despises form, for a work endures by that alone." It may be well imagined, therefore, that some of the more daringly amorphous productions of certain poets of the modern school who take pride in having emancipated themselves from the trammels of metrical restraint, find small favour with Monsieur France. " They had a grace of their own," he says of the poetical effusions of Jeanne Lefuel, a young actress whom he loved for a year in his youth, and who had a trick of adorning the doors of her lodgings with verses framed in a border of flowers painted in water colours, " they had a grace of their own, but they exhibited metrical defects that used to shock me; *those defects would pass unnoticed nowadays;* we live in a different age."

Next to Form, Monsieur France insists on the importance of balance, of *mesure*, of a just sense of proportion and, no less, on brevity. Manifold and exacting are the occupations of mankind and "brevity is the primary courtesy, *la première politesse*, demanded of the writer towards people of intelligence whose time is occupied and who know the value of the hours." Hence his predilection for the short story, which he calls *l'élixir et la quintessence*, *l'onguent précieux*. Like Renan, he fought shy of eloquence. "Let us beware of writing too well," he says; "it is the worst possible manner of writing." An Attic, he shunned all inappropriate heightening of tone, as a gentleman shrinks from vulgar display in his attire. *Il sait garder la mesure ;* he keeps a due sense of proportion. For the scholar, his prose exhales a perfume of antiquity. It is fragrant with the thyme of Hymettus, with the roses of Pæstum. It possesses a noble familiarity, a comely grace, and it moves without effort.

Vera incessu patuit dea . . .

Because Monsieur France aims at an austere elegance, a classic purity of style, at a use of words, that is to say, which is impregnated with beauty, which is illumined from within rather than bedizened with adventitious ornament, it is natural

that he should have early disdained the Romantics
to whom, in his youth, he was so ardently attached.
The verbose, the redundant, the flamboyant, the
pretentious, all these things he learned to shun,
and we even find him talking of the windy bombast
of that Demigod of the Romantics, Monsieur Victor
Hugo, to whom he was, clearly, not at all drawn.
" There was," he said, " too much of a din going
on in the great man's own head, for him to catch
any whispers from the ' passèd world.'" This is,
perhaps, a little unkind; and when we find him
describing the demi-god's romanticism as " un
formidable et vain assemblage de mots "—how
impossible to convey to English ears the faintly
mocking suggestion of that " formidable "—it is
evident that a marked antipathy existed between
the youthful Parnassian and the tumultuous genius
whom that school regarded, rather strangely we
admit, as their titular chief; evident that, even
then, he had come, like Monsieur Duvergier de
Hauranne, to look on romanticism as a disease
resembling epilepsy or walking in one's sleep. Why
he should have been so severe with Victor Hugo
and so tender with Lamartine and Musset seems
obscure, but there is an explanation. According
to Anatole France, Victor Hugo could not, or at
all events did not, depict human beings. " It is a
sad and rather disquieting thing that, amid all his

enormous output, amid all the monstrous beings he created, one never finds a single human face. The secret of hearts was never completely revealed to him. He was not made to love and to understand." And most piquant of paradoxes, rather than from Victor Hugo, rather than from any lord of language, classic or romantic, this master of the polished phrase, this scholar who wore the mantle of his erudition with such careless ease and unassuming grace, sought the foundations of his style far otherwhere. " From the lips of my old nurse," he says, " I learnt sound, honest French. Mélanie's speech was the speech of the peasantry, it smacked of the countryside. From her lips there flowed the light, limpid diction of our forefathers. Not knowing how to read, she pronounced her words as she had heard them as a child, and they from whom she had learned them were untutored folk who spoke as with the voice of Nature herself. And thus it was that Mélanie's way of talking was both natural and seemly. Words as rich in colour and as full of savour as the fruits of our orchards came to her without effort." In literature as in life, a little infusion of peasant stock is a salutary protection against the consequences of too much in-breeding.

Anatole France has the true philologist's passion for words, for tracing their origin, for noting the modifications they have undergone, for restoring

the edge to those that have been blunted by
inaccurate usage. His knowledge of his language
and its history is as wide as his love for it is deep.
What an armoury he possesses for the confusion of
the Brid'oisons of his day. " A pédant, pédant et
demi ! " exclaimed Figaro on a well known occasion,
and woe to any Dryasdust who should be rash
enough to try conclusions with Monsieur Anatole
France. His learning is prodigious ; yet his poise,
his philosophic balance is never disturbed or over-
weighted by it. He sees life steadily and he sees
it whole. With the insight of genius he can enter
into the state of mind and speak with the tongue
appropriate to all his characters from the highest to
the lowest, scholar, politician, priest, soldier, voluptuary, wanton, all the motley *dramatis personæ* that
move across the stage of life. Here, for example,
is a page which Bossuet might have penned. It is
an analysis of the *Origines du Christianisme :* " Ce
livre nous découvre dans l'humilité même du
christianisme la cause de son triomphe. Rome
étend sa puissance bienfaisante sur tout le monde
connu. Plus grande dans la paix que dans la guerre
elle administre les provinces avec une souveraine
sagesse." [1] But there is a people whom she has

[1] This book reveals to us in the very lowliness of the Christian
religion the causes of its triumph. Rome extends its beneficent
sway over the whole of the known world. Greater in peace than
in war she governs her provinces with sovereign wisdom. . . .

despised and rejected. "Ils sont la lie de l'humanité, le rebut des peuples, ces Juifs du Janicule. Dans leur abjection et leur dénuement, ils n'ont que leurs rêves. Ce sont leurs rêves qui changeront le monde. De l'infame Suburre, des ergastules, des carrières, des prisons, va sortir l'Église que Constantin fera asseoir dans la pourpre, qui arrachera de la Curie la statue de la Victoire et qui, debout sur les ruines de Rome, disputera l'empire aux Césars germains et se fera baiser les pieds par les rois et les empereurs."[1]

With that majestic passage, compare this that might have come from Maupassant: "Quand la femme à Robertet, la grande Léocadie, paya une paire de bretelles à son valet pour l'amener à faire ce qu'elle voulait qu'il fît, elle ne fut si fine que Robertet ne s'avisa du manège. Il surprit les galants au bon moment et corrigea sa femme à coups de chambrière si rudement qu'elle perdit à jamais l'envie de recommencer. Et, depuis lors, Léocadie est une des meilleures femmes de la contrée; son mari n'a pas ça a lui reprocher. C'est aussi qu'il

[1] "They are the dregs of humanity, the outcasts of the nations, these Jews of the Janicular. Downtrodden and naked, they have naught left them save their dreams. But those dreams are to change the face of the world. From the infamous Suburra, from workhouse and hovel and gaol shall come forth the Church which Constantine will clothe in purple, which shall snatch the statue of Victory from the Curia and which, erect, upon the ruins of Rome, shall dispute the supreme power with the German Cæsars and give its feet to be kissed by Kings and by Emperors."

faut marcher droit avec M. Robertet qui a de la
conduite et sait mener les bêtes et les gens." [1]

But the grace and music of his style are found
in their most unrivalled perfection in those passages,
reflective, descriptive or elegiac, in which, speaking
with his own voice, he dwells on some aspect of his
beloved country, or lingers in meditative compassion over the sufferings and sorrows of the poor
and lowly. Listen to the description of the burial
of a little fisher boy of Saint Valery who had been
drowned in the bay :

" Le cortège entra sous les vieux porches et
l'office des morts commença. Derrière le cercueil,
au poêle blanc dont les cordons étaient tenus par
quatre petits garçons raidement habillés de gros
drap noir, le père et la mère se tenaient par le bras.
L'homme ne pleurait plus. Mais on voyait que
les larmes avaient coulé longtemps sur le cuir fauve
de ses joues. La tête renversée, il sanglotait. Les
sanglots secouaient son long collier de barbe grise

---

[1] " When Robertet's wife, big Léocadie, paid for a pair of
braces for her manservant in order to induce him to do what she
wanted him to do, she was not so clever that Robertet did not
find out her little game. He caught the lovers in the very act,
and gave his wife such a sound thrashing with a horsewhip that
she lost all desire to sin again for ever and ever. Since then
Léocadie has been one of the best wives in the country-side. Her
husband hasn't *that* to find fault with her for. You see you've
got to run straight with M. Robertet. He knows what he's about
and how to handle people and animals."

et ses hautes épaules. Ils donnaient à sa bouche un faux air de sourire horrible à voir. Cependant il se balançait ainsi qu'un homme ivre et il mêlait aux chants des psaumes et aux prières de l'officiant une plainte lente, régulière et douce, comme l'air d'une de ces chansons avec lesquelles on endort les petits enfants. Ce n'était qu'un murmure, et l'église en était pleine ! Mais elle, la mère ! debout, immobile, muette dans sa pelisse antique, elle tenait son capuchon baissé au dessous de sa bouche, et sous ce voile elle amassait sa douleur.

Quand l'absoute fut donnée, le cortège s'achemina vers Cayeux. C'est là, sous le vent de mer, qu'ils veulent que leur enfant repose. Croient-ils que cette terre, si dure aux vivants, sera douce aux morts ? Ou plutôt n'est-ce pas qu'ils gardent un tendre amour pour le rude pays où ils sont nés et auquel ils portent aujourd'hui ce qu'ils avaient de plus cher ? Nous vîmes la petite troupe disparaître lentement sur le chemin pierreux. Jamais pour ma part, je n'avais contemplé un si grand spectacle. C'est qu'il n'y a rien de plus grand au monde que la douleur. Dans les villes, elle se cache. Aujourd'hui je l'ai vue au soleil sur une colline qui ressemblait au calvaire." [1]

[1] "The procession passed in beneath the ancient porch, and the burial service began. Four little boys, stiffly dressed in coarse black cloth suits, acted as pall bearers. Behind stood the

That passage from the words " Quand l'absoute fut donnée " to the end it would be difficult to rival, impossible, even from Monsieur France's own writings, to surpass.

Here is a picture of twilight, near Siena, on the wild and lonely road to Monte Oliveto :

" Les cloches de la ville sonnaient la mort tranquille du jour, et la pourpre du soir tombait avec

---

father and mother holding each other's arm. The man was not weeping now, but you could see how the tears had been streaming down his weather-beaten cheeks. His head was bowed and he was sobbing convulsively. His sobs shook his grey beard that hung like a scarf beneath his chin; they shook his high shoulders and imparted a sort of unnatural smile to his mouth, ghastly to behold. All the time he was swaying and tottering like a drunken man and he joined in the psalms and in the prayers in monotonous moaning tones, measured and low, like one of those airs with which mothers croon their little ones to sleep. It was but a murmur, yet it filled the church. It was otherwise with the mother. Upright, motionless, silent in her antique pelisse, her hood drawn down to the chin, she stood hoarding her grief apart. After the absolution the procession set out towards Cayeux. For it was there, with the salt winds streaming over him, that they wished their dear child to be laid to rest. Did they deem that the earth there, so harsh to the living, would be gentle to the dead; or was it rather that they held in their hearts a tender love for the stubborn soil that had borne them and to which they were carrying all that was dearest to them in the world? We stood and watched the little band wind slowly out of sight along the rough stony road. Never in my life had I beheld a scene so grand. For, in truth, there is nothing in the world so grand as sorrow. In towns sorrow is hidden away, hugger-mugger, out of sight, but to-day I beheld it in the broad open sunlight, on a hill that looked like a Calvary."

une majesté mélancolique sur la chaîne basse des collines. Quand déjà les noirs escadrons des corneilles avaient gagné les remparts, seul dans le ciel d'opale, un épervier tournait, les ailes immobiles, au-dessus d'une yeuse isolée. J'allais au devant du silence, de la solitude et des douces épouvantes qui grandissaient devant moi. Insensiblement la marée de la nuit recouvrait la campagne. Le regard infini des étoiles clignait au ciel. Et dans l'ombre, les mouches de feu faisait palpiter sur les buissons leur lumière amoureuse. . . ." [1]

And here is a passage which in its lightness and grace recalls Renan and which yet is not Renan, but Anatole France and no other : " La source qui descendait le coteau feuillu où le Pieux Valery s'arrêta était une des sources sacrées auxquelles ces hommes faisaient des offrandes. Elle coule encore au pied de la Chapelle, du côté de la baie. Comme aux anciens jours, l'eau en est fraîche et toute claire.

[1] " The church bells knelled the peaceful ending of the day, while the purple shades of night descended sadly and majestically on the low chain of neighbouring hills. The black squadrons of the rooks had already sought their nests about the city walls, but relieved against the opalescent sky, a single sparrow hawk still hung floating with motionless wings above a solitary ilex tree. I moved forward to confront the silence and solitude and the mild terrors that lowered before me in the growing dusk. The tide of darkness rose by imperceptible degrees and drowned the landscape. The infinite of starry eyes winked in the sky, while in the gloom below, the fire-flies spangled the bushes with their trembling love-lights."

LA BÉCHELLERIE

Showing the Fountain and the Front Door.   From a photograph by M. Henry Davray

Mais maintenant elle ne chante plus. Elle n'est
plus libre comme au temps de sa rustique divinité.
On l'a emprisonnée dans une cuve de pierre à
laquelle on accède par plusieurs degrés. Du temps
de Saint Valery, c'était une nymphe. Nulle main
n'avait osé la retenir, elle fuyait sous les saules.
Semblable à ces ruisseaux qu'on voit encore en
grand nombre dans les vallées du pays, elle formait,
de distance en distance, de petits lacs où sommeillait,
sur un lit flottant de feuilles vertes, la pâle fleur
du nénuphar." [1]

Great artists in words fall, roughly, into two
classes; those who appeal to the inward eye and
those who appeal to the inward ear. Flaubert, for
example, attaches such importance to rhythm that,
according to Monsieur Albert Thibaudet "il lui
fallait faire passer plusieurs fois ses phrases par la
preuve sonore," he tested the sound of his sentences

---

[1] "The brook which babbled down the leafy hillside, where
the pious St. Valery ceased his wanderings, was one of those sacred
streams to which these men of old made offering. It still flows
on by the walls of the chapel on the seaward side. Just as in the
olden days, it is cold and clear as crystal. But its song is hushed.
It is no longer free as in the days of its rustic divinity. It has
been caught and imprisoned in a stone basin with a flight of steps
leading up to it. In Saint Valery's day that stream was a nymph.
No hand had dared restrain her as she glanced away beneath the
willows. Like the rivulets of which there are so many in the
valleys round about, the stream broadened out here and there
into little lakes, where, upborne upon a floating couch of green
leaves, slumbered the pale blossom of the water lily."

over and over again. More .than this, he carried
the music of what he was going to write in his head,
long before he set it down on paper. The *Journal
des Goncourt* records Gautier as saying, " What do
you think Flaubert said to me the other day :
' It's finished, I've got another ten pages to write,
but I've got all my phrase-endings.' (*J'ai toutes
mes chutes de phrases*). He meant that he had got
the music of his sentences in his head before he had
written them. Il a ses chutes, que c'est drôle !
hein ? " So, too, like Flaubert, we can imagine
Monsieur France revolving in his mind the music
of his incomparable pages, for, while the prose of
some writers is, essentially, pictorial or sculpturesque
or architectural, the prose of Anatole France is,
essentially, musical. With him the accent, the
march, the movement is all-important, and the
translator, if he would retain some faint hint of
the magic of the original, must bear this perpetually
in mind. It is an exercise, and how difficult an
exercise, in the art of verbal orchestration.

Yes, the all-important factor in Anatole France's
prose is its music. And what music it is ! He
reminds one of some great and tender-hearted
violinist drawing from his instrument strains that
awaken all the emotions of the human heart. It
is unique and *sui generis ;* a music unheard before,
a music that none other will ever be able to repro-

duce. It can be grave or gay, ironic or compassionate, persuasive or indignant, dignified or familiar, learned or simple. It glows with the serene beauty of the classics, and, at its best, it is incomparable and unsurpassed.

R

AT LA BÉCHELLERIE

EARLY in May, 1923, I was staying in Paris with my friend Henry Davray and, together with him, I called on Anatole France one afternoon at the Villa Saïd. The Master had come up to Paris for a few days to witness the performance at the Odéon of a dramatized version of *Les Dieux ont Soif*. It happened that our call took place on the eve of his departure for Touraine, and many friends had come to take their leave of him. Both Monsieur and Madame France received us with the friendliest courtesy, but anything in the nature of a *tête-à-tête* was, in the circumstances, out of the question. Madame France with a kindness for which we owe her a lasting obligation, learning that we intended to remain in France some days longer, suggested that we should visit them at La Béchellerie, an invitation which we eagerly accepted. A day or so later we took the train to Tours, and thus it was that I made my first acquaintance with one of the loveliest and most fertile provinces of " la douce France."

A softly undulating plain, rich in vineyards and
all manner of fruit trees, then at the very height
of their passionate blossoming; here and there white
houses, half manor, half farm, gleaming delicate as
lace-work amid the whispering shadows of their
sheltering poplars; the fresh green of the spring-
tide, tenderer and more virginal from the lightness
of the soil here, that soil which imparts a keenness
and, withal, a delicacy to the wines of Touraine
which even the famed vineyards of the Bordelais
are unable to surpass; the silver-blue waters of the
Loire bejewelled with towered cities and stately
châteaux whose very names — Blois, Amboise,
Chenonceaux, Azay-le-Rideau—apart from the
historic memories they awaken, fall like music on the
ear—such is the scene amid which Anatole France,
now in the evening of his days, seeks refreshment and
repose from the more formal and exacting life of the
metropolis.

There is an airy, almost unsubstantial grace which
distinguishes everything in this favoured region.
The hearts of the men and women here in this district
of Touraine seem merrier, their mien more alert,
their step more buoyant than elsewhere. Some
would attribute this gaiety to the quality of the
wines grown hereabout, and truly a certain Vouvray,
which we drank beneath the dappled shade of a
gigantic plane tree beside an auberge not far from

Amboise, would seem a sovereign remedy against
Melancholy and all her dark-stoled retinue. But
apart from the wine, there is a clarity, a sparkle, an
Attic purity in the atmosphere which, I fancy, com-
municates itself to the hearts and minds of the
people

The sun was pouring down with all the brilliance
of a precocious May day when, leaving, soon after
noon, the city of Tours, whose cathedral towers
stretch, like two arms, imploringly heavenwards, we
drove out over the bridge that spans the broad,
swift-flowing waters of the Loire and mounted the
steep incline that leads to Monsieur France's country
home.   When we had reached the summit, our way
lay for a distance of three or four hundred yards
along a lane flanked by cornfields and vineyards and
orchards with, here and there, a grange over whose
garden wall the tamarisk drooped its mauve-pink
tresses ; then, as we turned sharply to the left,
a shady avenue brought us to a garden in the midst
of which was a fountain surmounted by a nymph,
and there before us rose up the graceful outlines of
La Béchellerie.

We mounted the steps that led to the entrance.
The door was open, and as we gazed across the white,
spacious hall, cool and almost cloistral in its simplicity, we saw the Master standing on the terrace
that overlooks the garden at the rear of the house.

The inevitable red skull-cap was pushed back over his head, and, attired in a suit of darkish tweed, he was apparently giving directions to his men concerning the planting of some shrubs. We hesitated for a moment whether to ring the bell, or to go forward unannounced. We had just decided on the bolder course when the Master turned and advanced to greet us. Ten years—for it was a decade since I, at least, had seen him—ten years, whereof five had been overhung with the sombre tragedy of war, had left, I thought, but little trace upon him. The eyes yet smiled their gravely humorous smile, and the voice in which he bade us welcome to La Béchellerie had lost none of its musical sonorousness. Madame France now came to add her welcome to her husband's.

The first formal words of greeting over, I found myself pacing the garden walk side by side with the Master. Up to that point I had felt naturally and I hope becomingly shy; so much so that the speech which I had anxiously premeditated as I lay awake in the small hours of the morning and of which I had fondly hoped to throw off with the easy, careless air of an impromptu, had gone beyond recall. Nevertheless, I was surprised to find myself quite unabashed. The " Great Man " of whom I had felt so much in awe as the hour of my visit approached, had miraculously given place to the

" Friend " whom I had learned to love long ago
when I translated *Le Livre de Mon Ami* into English. And so, instead of the speech on which I
had so confidently relied and which had so completely, and perhaps fortunately, forsaken me, I
found myself talking, strangely and unaccountably
at my ease, about Virgil. How it came about, I
cannot now remember. It may have been the
peacefulness of the scene, the calm that seemed to
rest like a benediction upon the fields, which brought
into my mind that poet who had so deep a love of
the country, and of country life and the deep peace
which it offers :

Secura quies et nescia fallere vita.

Anyhow Virgil was the theme, and the Master, who
knows his Virgil by heart, recited or rather intoned
line after line with a fervour that lent a new beauty
to the familiar words. When, at length, we turned
our steps again towards the house, he stooped and
plucked a flower. I had produced a little pocket
Virgil, which I happened to have with me, and the
Master, turning towards me with a smile, half-
humorous, half-sad, bade me open it at his favourite
passage. Standing with uplifted hand he declaimed
those lines in the Sixth Æneid in which the poet
describes the Grove of Myrtle amid whose shadows
wander for evermore those hapless ones who are

consumed, even in death, by the pangs of hopeless
love, among whom the Trojan hero descries
Phœnician Dido " even as a man sees, or thinks he
has seen, the moon rising amid the clouds when
the month is young."

> "*Hic quos durus amor . . .*"

he recited, and when I had found the place, he
gently laid the flower he had gathered, upon the
page. It was a memorable little incident. The
" careless ordered garden " flooded with golden
sunlight, the distinguished-looking old man with his
grey beard and his quaint crimson cap, his enigmatic
smiling eyes, his fine expressive hands, and then the
little simple, unaffected, but strangely gracious act,
almost feminine in its delicacy. It was a picture I
shall not forget.

It would take too long to recount even a little
of the memorable things he said to me during my
visit. Comparing Racine and Shakespeare he said,
" Racine's murderers are monsters, præterhuman,
they excite our horror, whereas Shakespeare's—
Macbeth, Hamlet, Othello and the rest—awaken our
sorrow, appeal to our pity, and we weep for them."
Virgil, Homer, the Greek dramatists, literary style,
the art of translation, were some of the subjects on
which we touched, and then the talk drifted, or
seemed to drift—for to speak frankly I think Henry

Davray subtly directed it—into French politics. Being but a mediocre politician I was but " mute and audience to this act." As everybody knows, Anatole France is a resolute and uncompromising opponent of war. " Wars," he said, " are both criminal and useless, and they do but sow the seed of endless discord. Yet a man can always attain a little transient popularity by inciting the masses to pursue a policy of violence. To wave a flag and beat a drum is a pretty sure way to office; but the reckoning comes sooner or later, and it is usually a bitter one."

" In England," I said, " people are asking how it comes about that you, who so long played the part of an amused and rather ironic spectator of life, commenting upon the human drama with something of the remoteness, the detachment of the chorus in a Greek play, should at last have quitted your Tower of Ivory to descend into the arena and identify yourself with a definite political party."

" If your friends are asking that," said the Master, " then tell them when you get home, to go and read their *Don Quixote*."

" Do you mean," said I, " that you feel you are attempting the impossible, and that here, too, all is illusion ? "

The Master made no answer.

" I will say that, if you wish," I said, " but what

I had it in my heart to tell them, was that you, too, put on your armour and buckled on your sword to strike a blow for Dreyfus, and that never since then have you wearied in the fight against the powers of injustice and intolerance. I was going to tell them that, though you hate war, you, too, are a soldier, and that you will never cease to do battle against tyranny and injustice."

"That, too, you may tell them," said the old man with rather a sad smile. "That, too, for I hope, nay, I think, it is not untrue."

That the Master still preserves his playful humour, despite his eighty years, the following little incident will show.

"It is a very salutary thing," I said jokingly, while Madame poured the tea, "for me to spend a few days from time to time with my friend Davray. His opinions are clear and definite. Everything he sees is either black or white; whereas I am only too prone, like a certain Pierre Nozière, to go a-dreaming and to set a note of interrogation after all my ideas."

The Master smiled. "And you, mademoiselle," he said to a young lady who was present, "whose side are you on; ours or Monsieur Davray's?"

Mademoiselle paused for several seconds, and then being pressed again for an answer, she said, rather timidly, "I do not know. I am afraid I cannot make up my mind."

" Then," exclaimed the Master triumphantly,
" it is clear you are on the side of the doubters :
you are on our side."

After tea, Monsieur France showed us over the
house, which is noteworthy and beautiful enough to
merit a detailed description.

La Béchellerie dates from the reign of Louis
XIII, that is to say, from the early part of the seventeenth century. It is in the purest style of the
period and has suffered no disfigurement at the
hands of the restorer. The exterior is delightful
in its elegant simplicity, the wings symmetrically
and harmoniously disposed. The windows, the
lines of which are of great beauty, are sufficiently
large to afford ample light to the spacious chambers
within. From the hall, an easy staircase, adorned
with wrought-iron balusters of singularly graceful
design, leads to the single upper storey.

On the southern side of the house a sunny terrace
overlooks the flower garden, to which access is given
by a flight of stone steps. To the right an avenue
of close-clipped limes with tufted foliage affords a
grateful shade. To the left, beside an ancient
wall stands a lofty stone-built Renaissance pavilion
or summer-house, which the Master has caused to
be fitted with shelves in order to house the overflow
from his library in Paris.

The principal entrance to the house is on the

northern side. A short carriage drive leaves the
high road at right angles, and two wide gates of
solid wood give access to a spacious garden court.
A broad carriage-way girdles a trim lawn, in the
midst of which is a fountain where the lotus blooms
amid the soft spray that falls from a pedestal surmounted by the stone figure of a startled nymph.
Low down, along the edge of the fountain pool,
stand stone vases of the purest design. Visitors who
come upon La Béchellerie by way of this garden
court find it difficult to restrain a cry of admiration,
so elegant, so stately, yet withal so simple, is the
aspect of the home the Master has chosen.

Within the house, the *salons*, great and small,
the dining-room, the sitting-rooms and the guest-
chambers, all contain antique furniture selected with
unerring taste. The bedroom of Madame France,
with its four-post bed and azure hangings, recalls
those sleeping apartments of queens and princesses,
which are displayed to the visitor in the Royal
palaces of olden days. The Master's bedroom is in
a graver style, but each piece of furniture is of
ancient date and of the purest and most gracious
simplicity. Nothing harsh, nothing morose, could
find a place amid such artistic perfection. From
window and terrace the eye ranges with delight over
the soft outline of the valleys, over hills covered with
vines, over wooded heights, over fields of corn and

clover. No sharp jagged horizon is here, but wave upon wave of tilth and vineyard as far as eye can see.

As I stood beside him gazing out over the peaceful smiling scene, I said that somehow it made me think of that beautiful line in the English liturgy, "The peace of God which passeth all understanding."

Putting his hand on my shoulder he said, "Je ne suis pas croyant (I am not a believer), but there are passages of wonderful, poignant beauty in the Catholic liturgy," and in his low musical voice he recited some passages from the Roman missal.

Returning once more to the drawing-room, Monsieur France continued to talk with great animation. I had one more favour to ask him, and that was that he would read aloud a page of his own writings. He readily assented—he said, with a laugh, that he could refuse us nothing—and asked me what he should read. I chose a certain passage from *Pierre Nozière*, quoted on page 238 of this book.

"That," I said, "is a passage to set beside the opening paragraph of Renan's *Souvenirs d'Enfance et de Jeunesse*. It seems to me that in both cases the perfection of prose is achieved."

"No," said Anatole France, "not so. Not in both cases, for Renan at his best is unsurpassed and unsurpassable. . . ."

A GROUP AT THE ENTRANCE TO THE LIBRARY AT LA BÉCHELLERIE

From left to right the four central figures are: Lucien Psichari, J. Lewis May,
Anatole France, Madame France (seated)

From a photograph by M. Henry Davray

The shadows were lengthening as the gracious old man came with us to the porch of his house to bid us a smiling good-night.

Looking out from the window of our car as we passed rapidly through the gates of La Béchellerie, we caught a glimpse of our host standing at the doorway of his house gaily waving his crimson cap.

There is a strange, rather pathetic dignity about this old man passing his days of quiet in this sequestered manor of Touraine, finding solace in his garden and his books, surrounded by the tender but unobtrusive ministrations of those who are dearest to him, his wife and his young grandson Lucien Psichari, whose father, the husband of Anatole France's daughter, died heroically in the Great War, and in whose veins there flows the blood of another of France's greatest writers—Ernest Renan. Often he will go down into the city of Tours, which, besides the air of calm and beautiful antiquity which broods upon it like a charm, presents to a bibliophile like Anatole France, this additional and cardinal attraction : a most excellent bookshop presided over by a prince among booksellers, the genial and hospitable Monsieur Tridon. The librairie Tridon—it recalls the librairie Paillot of the Bergeret series—is the rendezvous of the *beaux esprits* of the neighbourhood.

" Do you know," said Monsieur France, " that

when I go there I always meet a red-hot royalist and that he and I are great friends?

"I am rather like a certain Justice of the Peace I once knew. He was a tremendous anti-clerical. Yet he got on admirably with the village curé and also with the schoolmaster. 'Well,' he used to say, 'it's like this, you see; we are the only three "messieurs" in the place.'"

What, one wonders, are the memories that steal into his mind there, now that he has put off his heavy armour. We, who have read *The Bloom of Life*, and its three predecessors, know how he loves to dwell on the days of his childhood, how tenderly and with what a sense of living reality he recalls his home, first on the Quai Malaquais and then on the Quai Voltaire; his father, dignified, opinion-ated, looking down a little patronizingly—for was he not the compiler of the *Catalogue de la Bedoyère?* —on the intellectual capabilities of his women folk; his mother, devout, church-going, but very alert, very practical, very "busy about the house"; and all those others, grandmother, god-parents, friends and servants, whom he has portrayed so vividly. Then, doubtless, there pass before his mind his early days at Lemerre's; the tumultuous gatherings of the Parnassians; his experiences in the Senate Library; and then his first books, the praise that they awakened; the gradual but certain establish-

ment of his fame ; next, the fulfilment of the French
man of letters' crowning ambition, his election to the
Academy ; and then the tragic Dreyfus case, the
five years' nightmare of the Great War, and now,
at length, tranquillity and the homage of the whole
cultured world offered to him here in the very heart
of his beloved land, in Touraine, whose very name
lingers in the mind like airy music, evoking as by
some mysterious charm, the bright and gracious
spirit of the land and people of France.   Truly his
reveries should bring him pride and consolation.
Though his pen and the mind that guides it are
as unfaltering as ever, it is probable that he will write
but little more ; and when his voice is hushed, we
shall never listen to such music again.   No one will
ever speak quite as he has spoken.   It is the fate of
writers of genius, at once to inspire imitation and to
render imitation impossible.   Their works bear the
impress of an inalienable and incommunicable
individuality.   However diligently we analyse their
style, however eagerly we seek to capture and isolate
the subtle quality in their work which gives it its
permanence and its charm, in the end the finer
essence eludes us.   We may know well enough what
we mean when we speak of the Virgilian quality of a
passage of poetry, or the Shakespearean, or the Mil-
tonic, but we cannot define it in words ; still less
can we reproduce it.   We may study the prosody

of these poets with unwearying and ingenious minuteness, . yet, in the last resort, we can but describe them in terms of themselves, and, as Virgil is Virgil, Shakespeare Shakespeare, Milton Milton, so Anatole France is Anatole France and no other. Those who have felt the spell of Anatole France and are conscious of his peculiar charm know instinctively that such accents will never fall upon their ears again. There will doubtless be born other writers whose work will be no less illumined by grace and beauty, but it will be a different grace, a different beauty. And the reason perhaps is that Anatole France, in nearly all his writings, certainly in all those by which he will be chiefly held in memory, expresses himself, his individuality—his *ego*, rather than ideas external to himself. He gives utterance not so much to the results of some intellectual process, but to the dictates of his whole nature, heart and mind indissolubly interwoven, and, if the language he employs is the language of France, his voice is the voice of all humanity.

APPENDIX

THE works of Anatole France to which reference is made in this book, together with the dates of publication. Where translations exist, the English title is also given.

1868. Alfred de Vigny.
1873. Les Poèmes Dorés.
1876. Les Noces Corinthiennes. (The Bride of Corinth.)
1879. Jocaste et Le Chat Maigre. (Jocasta and The FamishedCat.)
1881. Le Crime de Sylvestre Bonnard. (The Crime of Sylvestre Bonnard.)
1882. Les Désirs de Jean Servien. (The Aspirations of Jean Servien.)
1885. Le Livre de Mon Ami. (My Friend's Book.)
1888–92. La Vie Littéraire. (On Life and Letters.)
1889. Balthasar. (Balthasar.)
1890. Thaïs. (Thaïs).
1892. L'Étui de Nacre. (Mother of Pearl.)
1893. La Rôtisserie de la Reine Pédauque. (At the Sign of the Reine Pédauque.)
        Les Opinions de M. Jérôme Coignard. (The Opinions of Jérôme Coignard.)
1894. Le Lys Rouge. (The Red Lily.)
1895. Le Jardin d'Épicure. (The Garden of Epicurus.)
        Le Puits de Sainte-Claire. (The Well of St. Clare.)
1897. Le Mannequin d'Osier. (The Wickerwork Woman.)
        L'Orme du Mail. (The Elm Tree on the Mall.)
1899. L'Anneau d'Améthyste. (The Amethyst Ring.)
        Pierre Nozière. (Pierre Nozière.)
1900. Clio. (Clio.)
1901. Monsieur Bergeret à Paris. (Monsieur Bergeret in Paris.)

S   257

1903. Histoire Comique. (A Mummer's Tale.)
1904. Crainquebille, Putois Riquet, etc. (Crainquebille.)
1905. Sur la Pierre Blanche. (The White Stone.)
1908. L'Ile des Pingouins. (Penguin Island.)
   La Vie de Jeanne d'Arc. (The Life of Joan of Arc.)
1909. Les Contes de Jacques Tournebroche. (The Merrie Tales of Jacques Tournebroche.)
   Les Sept Femmes de la Barbe-Bleue. (The Seven Wives of Bluebeard.)
1912. Les Dieux ont Soif. (The Gods are Athirst.)
1913. Le Génie Latin. (The Latin Genius.)
1914. La Révolte des Anges. (The Revolt of the Angels.)
1915. Sur la Voie Glorieuse. (The Path of Glory.)
1918. Le Petit Pierre. (Little Pierre.)
1922. La Vie en Fleur. (The Bloom of Life.)

INDEX